Forex Trading - 3 Hour Crash Course

Master the Basics of Currency Investing in a Few Hours: A Beginner's Guide

Edward Day

© Copyright 2020 - All rights reserved.

The content contained within this book may not be reproduced, duplicated or transmitted without direct written permission from the author or the publisher.

Under no circumstances will any blame or legal responsibility be held against the publisher, or author, for any damages, reparation, or monetary loss due to the information contained within this book, either directly or indirectly.

Legal Notice:

This book is copyright protected. It is only for personal use. You cannot amend, distribute, sell, use, quote or paraphrase any part, or the content within this book, without the consent of the author or publisher.

Disclaimer Notice:

Please note the information contained within this document is for educational and entertainment purposes only. All effort has been executed to present accurate, up to date, reliable, complete information. No warranties of any kind are declared or implied. Readers acknowledge that the author is not engaged in the rendering of legal, financial, medical or professional advice. The content within this book has been derived from various sources. Please consult a licensed professional before attempting any techniques outlined in this book.

By reading this document, the reader agrees that under no circumstances is the author responsible for any losses, direct or indirect, that are incurred as a result of the use of the information contained within this document, including, but not limited to, errors, omissions, or inaccuracies.

Table of Contents

INTRODUCTION 1

FROM BEGINNER TO PROFESSIONAL 2
    Why Listen to Me? 5

CHAPTER 1: THE BASICS OF FOREX MARKETS 9

TIMINGS 9
    Sessions 11
    Market Structure 14
INSTRUMENTS 17
    Pairs 18
    Pips 25
    Derivatives 26

CHAPTER 2: BROKERS 29

MAKING MONEY IN FOREX 29
    Margin and Leverage 30
    Lots 32
    Pip Values 33
BROKER REGULATION 36
    Straight Through Processing 38
    Electronic Communication Network 38
    Dealing Versus Non Dealing 39
    Risk 41
SPREADS 43

CHAPTER 3: THE PRICE CHART 45

CANDLES AND BARS 45
    Structure 49
PRICE PATTERNS 52
    Pin Bars 53
    Two Bar Reversals 59

Engulfers	62

CHAPTER 4: SUPPORT AND RESISTANCE 67

SUPPORT AND RESISTANCE.. 67
    Swing Points 69
    Zones 71
    Strength... 73
    Higher Time Frames 76
    Reversals... 78
    Dynamic Levels 81
ORDER TYPES 83
    Market Orders 83
    Limit Orders 84
    Stop Orders... 86

CHAPTER 5: TECHNICAL INDICATORS 89

AVERAGE DIRECTIONAL INDEX 90
    How it Works 92
RELATIVE STRENGTH INDEX 95
    How it Works 97
PARABOLIC SAR 101
    How it Works 103
BOLLINGER BANDS 106
    How it Works 108

CHAPTER 6: RISK MANAGEMENT FOR BEGINNERS 111

WIN RATES.. 111
    Linear Thinking 112
    Success and Failure... 114
    Consistency... 117
    Risk of Ruin 120
    Amount or Percent 123

CHAPTER 7: THE TRADING MINDSET 127

WHY TRADING?.. 127
    Expectations 129
    Fear of Missing Out 132
HABITS.. 134

Preparation 135
Post-Trade Behavior 137

CHAPTER 8: SCALING 141

THE FIRST STEP 141
THE SECOND STEP 143
THE FINAL STEP 144

CONCLUSION 147

REFERENCES 149

Introduction

"Trading doesn't just reveal your character, it also builds it if you stay in the game long enough." - by Yvan Byeajee

If you've ever read anything to do with trading then odds are good that you've heard all about currencies and forex trading. FX trading as it's often referred to is different from stock trading in many ways and these distinctions are often lost on many traders. They jump into the forex market without paying any attention to the principles that govern the forex market and get burned.

Some traders go the opposite direction and stay away entirely from forex. They feel that the risks are far too high and that volatility and liquidity concerns are unmanageable. Then there's the newbie trader who knows nothing about stocks or forex or even the markets and simply wants to make money.

No matter which case applies to you, I'd like to extend you a warm welcome. You've made an excellent decision by purchasing this book. My aim in writing this book is to not just illuminate the wonderful world of forex trading for you but to also help you become a better trader. Forex market success often carries over into the stock market because the rigors of trading FX more often than not make one a better trader.

In addition to this the simple fact is that there is more money to be made in forex as compared to trading stocks. It's no secret that the stock markets around the world these days are dominated by high frequency algorithms that push prices too much in a given direction for the average retail trader to be able to make a profit.

Did you know that this is not the case in forex? This is just one of the many surprising things you will learn in this book.

From Beginner to Professional

This book is aimed at beginners to the forex market. When writing books of this nature, it is essential to make some assumptions. To include the highest number of people who can find this book useful, I've also assumed that most readers of this book will be beginners to trading as well. Even if you are a stock market trading expert, I urge you to take the time to read the sections on the basics of the forex market and about the instruments available since they function very differently to stocks.

Perhaps the biggest point of difference is the astronomical leverage you can access in the forex markets. Understanding and managing leverage is the key to your success since it both boosts your profits massively and creates losses that exceed multiples of your capital. A good forex trader understands that risk management is the key to success over the long term.

Let's get something clear right off the bat. It is easy to make money in forex. That's right! It really isn't difficult for you to have a string of profitable trades that will increase your account balance. What is tough is keeping that money you've made. The combination of leverage and easily spotted trading conditions have caused many a trader to blow up their accounts spectacularly.

The numbers are stark. According to a study conducted by the American Fx broker FXCM, 95% of accounts that are opened end up closing within a year due to a loss of capital (Rolf, 2020). Of the remaining 5%, only a small fraction last two years and an even smaller fraction end up remaining open for five years.

Mind you, retaining capital for five years is no guarantee of profits. Making money and keeping that money are two very different things when it comes to FX trading. Does this mean you should simply stick to stocks? Hardly.

For one thing, the degree to which the forex market moves is far greater than the movements you will see in the stock market. This is a very good thing for you as a trader since the further the market moves, the greater is your money making potential. Think of it this way: If something moves just 5 points a day, there's only so much money you can make.

If it were to move 100 points per day, you'd obviously make a lot more! This is pretty much what happens with the FX market when compared to the stock market. Learning how to take advantage of these movements is what this book is all about. You're going to start off by understanding what the forex market is and how different it is to the stock market.

You're then going to go on a deep dive and understand how forex currency instruments work. This is a very important chapter. If you cannot understand the instruments you're trading, you don't have much of a chance of success. You will also learn about the importance and danger of leverage and how you can use it wisely.

There are also some nuances with regards to brokers you need to understand when it comes to FX. You see, the forex brokerage space is a bit like the Wild West compared to the orderly small town that is stock market brokering. The rules are a bit different here and there are some shady practices you could fall victim to.

You're going to learn all about these and most importantly, how to protect yourself from them. Once this is done, you're going to learn how you can read price charts. Too many traders jump right into indicators and all sorts of fancy geometrical shapes and don't pay any attention to how price actually behaves.

You're going to learn an extremely simple method and some easy to spot patterns that will help you identify market conditions and will help you use the right indicators at the right time. Speaking of which you will also learn which indicators are the best to build a trading system around and why.

The fact is that many indicators don't work very well these days thanks to oversaturation but the key is to learn how to use them properly. Risk management and mindset are also important points that will be covered here and you need to incorporate these lessons into your trading strategy.

We'll end by looking at your trading plan and how you can build one in an optimal manner. Sounds good? The only thing left to address is your reasons for listening to me. There are many self-appointed gurus in this space so why are my words the ones you ought to listen to? I'm glad you asked!

Why Listen to Me?

At this point in my life, I am a full-time forex trader and I'm proud to say that it hasn't been an easy journey. You see, back when I started out, there were no books written about forex and there were no websites dedicated to providing you with trade signals or in-depth market research.

I was a regular guy with a degree in accounting, working as an accountant and being about as happy as an accountant can possibly be. In other words, I was bored out of mind with all the numbers I was crunching and my ability to get excited at the prospect of shifting expenses to capital expenditures was about spent.

One of my clients intrigued me immensely, since I had to audit his brokerage statements to calculate his profit and loss figures. I had seen many brokerage statements until that point in time but the stuff I saw here was nothing I could recognize. On further explanation he told me that he was a forex trader and urged me to attend a trading seminar he was attending in town.

Intrigued I went and it's safe to say that it got me hooked. I signed up for all the forex courses that were available at the time and was consumed by the market. My happiest moment occurred in 2008 when I could finally say goodbye to my full-time job and live off my trading. I currently am a guest speaker at many forex seminars across the country and mentor people looking to achieve success with their trading.

While forex is one of my passions, my deepest passion lies in my thirst for knowledge and in sharing everything I've learned. This is what motivated me to achieve success with forex in the first place. Despite having a natural inclination to be a trader, it was hard work that got me here.

I have no special talent and neither am I a genius. I'm just a guy much like you are. My persistence and unwillingness to give up is what brought me here and these are the same things that will fuel your success as well. As I said, you've made a great decision to pursue forex trading.

Now, it's time for you to go ahead and put some action behind that initial motivation. A world full of riches awaits you. Are you ready to work for it?

Chapter 1:

The Basics of Forex Markets

Before jumping into the exciting strategies to make money, you first need to understand the environment you'll be operating in. The forex market is a very different beast from its stock market cousin. While the principles of success remain largely the same in both, the underlying mechanics often create huge differences in the way the instruments in the markets behave.

The biggest difference or advantage that the forex market has is that it allows the trader to literally pick and choose when they want to trade. Let's begin by looking at how this is possible.

Timings

Stock markets around the world open and close at designated times. These are usually between eight to nine in the morning till four or five in the afternoon.

All trading is condensed into these hours. While there are after hours activities, the trading that takes place in these times is negligible compared to the volumes that the markets see during normal hours.

If you've traded the stock market before, you're probably familiar with the concept of sessions. A session is just a period of time in the market where certain trading characteristics occur. For example, in the American markets, the morning session is one of hectic activity and sees huge volumes. Then comes the afternoon session where everyone seemingly dozes off and volumes drop. Then comes the evening or closing session where volumes again rise.

The forex market also experiences this phenomenon of different sessions with one major difference: Sessions in forex comprise entire trading days. This is because the forex market does not close during the week. It is a 24-hour market that is always open. The only time it does close is on Friday night Pacific standard time. It reopens on Monday morning Auckland time (which is in the country of New Zealand).

In other words, the market is closed for just one day and is open the rest of the time. No matter what time of the day it is, you are assured of good trading volumes since someone somewhere is trading.

Sessions

The FX market is not localized like the stock market is. What I mean is that in order to trade American stocks, you will need to open an account with an American broker and place trades that will get sent to an American stock exchange. If you wish to trade Japanese stocks, you will need to send your order through a broker to a Japanese stock exchange.

This is not the case in forex. Imagine a market where all the stocks of the world traded on a single exchange. This is what the FX market is like. You're not trading stocks in the forex market but currency pairs. I'll explain these in more detail in the next chapter. For one, understand that Japanese currency pairs can be as freely traded as U.S Dollar currency pairs. You don't need to setup any special accounts to do this. A single forex trading account is more than enough to give you access to all instruments all around the world.

Thus, FX truly is a global market. As a result, the trading day is long and runs the entire 24-hour timespan. The forex trading day officially begins in Auckland, New Zealand and continues as Australia comes online. Following this, the Asian markets in Tokyo, Hong Kong and Singapore add to trading volumes. This is when the Asian session is in full swing.

As the day wears on in Tokyo and the rest of Asia, Western Europe begins to awake and the markets in Frankfurt, Geneva, Paris and Amsterdam come online and volumes surge. The last European market to open is London and the first two hours of the London session coincide with the final two hours of the market day in Asia. This period sees a lot of trading volumes since half the world's traders are online at this point in time.

As Asia closes, Europe marches forward with trading volumes remaining strong. Just as happened with Asia and Europe, as Europe begins to move into the evening, North America and specifically New York begins to come online. The final four hours of the trading day in London coincides with the first four hours of the trading day in New York.

Given that two of the biggest financial centres in the world are online, you would expect trading volumes to go through the roof and this is exactly what happens. This mini session, titled the New York/London overlap witnesses the highest volumes during the 24-hour forex market day.

London eventually winds down when it's lunch time in New York and volume subsides but remains relatively high throughout the New York trading day. Secondary American markets in Dallas and San Francisco come online and volumes receive a little boost. Eventually, New York closes.

During this portion of the FX day, none of the major markets are online and the market witnesses very low volumes until Auckland and Sydney wake up once again around midnight New York time. Eventually, Tokyo comes online and we go through the entire cycle once again.

The forex day can thus be divided into distinct sessions. There's the Asian session where the major markets in Asia and Oceania are open. The end of this session overlaps with the open of the European session which is powered primarily by London. The european session overlaps with the New York session where New York is the primary powerhouse driving volumes.

There is a gap between the New York close and the Asian open and there is no official name for this dead zone. Given the lack of traders taking part in it, it's perhaps appropriate that no one has bothered to give it a name. Every session has its own quirks that you'll understand better when we discuss foreex instruments.

Given that the market is always open and that you're not restricted in terms of the instruments you wish to trade, you're fully free to fire up your laptop and trade any instrument from anywhere at any point of the day. To trade successfully it helps to have a fixed routine but theoretically, you can fix your trade day at any point of the day and still make money.

This flexibility is missing in the stock market since there you're restricted to trading when the market is open. There is another huge difference between the two markets that you should be aware of and this is with regards to the way they're structured.

Market Structure

When you place an order in stocks, it travels from your broker to the stock exchange. The stock exchange matches your order with another order that it receives from somewhere else and stores this information in its records. This electronic record of your trade is called the order book.

Thus, the stock exchange at all times has an electronic record of all trades and transactions that are occuring within it during market hours. The FX market on the other hand doesn't work this way. FX operates via what is called an over the counter or OTC market. OTC markets exist in stocks as well but stock OTC markets carry different implications.

A stock trading OTC signifies that there isn;t much demand for it and that the number of active traders in that stock are very low. This is not what the FX market is. Instead, the term OTC is simply used to indicate that there isn't a centralized exchange or an order book system.

The FX market is actually a network of interbank dealers. These dealers are the major investment banks all around the world and they buy and sell currencies in the billions every single day. Different dealers might have expertise in different currencies. For example, if someone wishes to buy Japanese Yen, they're likely to contact a Japanese dealer rather than an Australian dealer.

Similarly, those looking to purchase the U.S Dollar will invariably contact a dealer based out of New York such as Citibank or Goldman Sachs. These banks have a network built up in between all of them. There is no restriction on who can be a dealer, it simply depends on who ends up transacting the most in various currencies. The higher the transaction volumes a dealer experiences, the greater is their stature in the network.

Every dealer is deeply connected to a few others in the larger network. As a result, a single interbank dealer does not have the full view of the volumes being traded in a particular currency. For example, a Japanese bank will know how much Yen it is transacting but it will not have a full picture of how much Yen another bank is trading throughout the day.

Neither will they have an idea of which currencies that Japanese Yen is being converted into. This is a classic decentralized market and as a result trading volumes are simply not known. This is in contrast to the stock market where volume data is always known thanks to the existence of the order book.

Thus, if you trade stocks using volume data in your strategies, these will not work in FX. This decentralized structure also has significant implications for algorithmic trading strategies. The rise of technology has led to the increased use of so called front running strategies in stock exchanges around the world.

Here's how it works: Let's say a huge investor decides to buy a few hundred million dollars worth of stock X.

If you could know this information beforehand and if you could buy that quantity of stock, you could very well increase the price of that stock by a few cents and sell it to that big investor.

Thanks to technological advances, a number of hedge funds can read the order book and figure out which stocks are witnessing increased demand. Before the orders from other investors can reach the exchange, they place buy orders and snap up whatever stock they can. They then turn around and sell this stock to the late arrivals at slightly marked up prices.

As a retail or small time trader, this will not impact you too much. However, it will cause odd behavior like your stop loss levels to be violated or you collecting slightly less profit than what you had hoped for. If you don't know what stop losses are then don't worry about this right now.

The point is that front running costs you money and it relies exclusively on there being a centralized order book. Since FX has no order book, there is nothing to front run. As a result, you will receive true prices more often than not if you trade through a reliable broker.

One step below the interbank dealers network are forex brokers. Forex brokers deserve their own chapter and in the next chapter you'll learn all about them. For now, let's take a look at the instruments that forex brokers will allow you to trade in.

Instruments

When it comes to the stock market, the primary instrument of trade is company stock. This is an easy instrument to understand. It represents the company in question and moves up and down based on market sentiment or the company's business prospects. Things aren't so straightforward when it comes to FX. For starters, there are no companies here, just currencies.

You might think that buying currencies outright is the way to go. For example, you could be thinking that you just buy the U.S Dollar and that's that. However, the dollar doesn't have any absolute value of its own like a company's stock does. Instead its value is derived based on its relationship to other currencies.

It could increase in value compared to the British Pound and decrease slightly against the Swiss Franc. So how would you compute your profit or loss if you simply bought the U.S Dollar? This would be impossible. This is why the instruments that are available to trade are currency pairs and not individual currencies themselves.

When you buy a forex currency pair, you're buying one currency and selling another. For example, one of the most heavily traded currency instruments in the world is the EURUSD. This is the currency pair between the Euro and the American Dollar. When you buy a unit of

EURUSD, you are buying Euros and selling Dollars simultaneously.

FX pairs have a base currency and a quote currency. In the EURUSD pair, the EUR is the base currency and the USD is the quote currency. The price of the pair indicates how much of the quote currency is needed to receive one unit of the base currency. For example, if the price of EURUSD is 1.234, this means that one Euro is equivalent to 1.234 USD.

Thus, as currency pair prices move up and down, you're really trading the exchange rates and not some absolute value of currency. You're looking to profit off the changes in the exchange rate between those two currencies.

Pairs

There are a large number of currency pairs. In fact, you could have a pair between pretty much every currency in the world. Despite this, there are a few pairs that receive the lion's share of trading volume. This is because the governments behind these currencies are stable and belong to developed economies where the chances of economic surprises are low.

All currency pairs belong to one of three categories: Major, minor and exotic. The following currency pairs belong to the major category:

- EURUSD - This is the most heavily traded currency pair in the world. Its peak trading volumes occur during the four hour overlap between the European and New York sessions. The pair itself is relatively stable in terms of movement (referred to as low volatility) and it only witnesses spikes in movement when there are major economic announcements.
- USDJPY- The U.S Dollar and Japanese Yen. This pair is also a heavily traded one but generally witnesses low volumes during the European session. Despite this, there are enough traders available to make a decent market of it (referred to as being liquid) at all times. The major spikes in volumes occur during the Asian session and the New York session.
- GBPUSD - This is the most volatile currency pair. The British Pound and the U.S Dollar largely mimics the movement of the EURUSD but in a far more exaggerated manner historically. With Brexit now a reality, this correlation has broken down further and the GBP has been extremely volatile during this decade thanks to political events. The pair is always liquid with spikes in volumes occuring during the European session and extends into the American session.

- AUDUSD - Also called the Aussie, this is the pair between the Aussie Dollar and the U.S Dollar. This pair is heavily dependent on the economic outlook in Australia which in turn is heavily dependent on whatever China is upto thanks to the close trade ties between both countries. The Aussie is a stable currency pair despite this and it is reliant on commodity prices since those are Australia's biggest export.
- USDCAD- This is the pair between the U.S Dollar and their beloved neighbors up north, Canada. Canad is a major oil producer so this is another pair that is heavily influenced by whatever is happening in the commodity markets. Given that both economies are in North America, trading them during the North American session makes the most sense.
- USDCHF- Commonly called the Swissie, this is the pair between the U.S Dollar and the Swiss Franc. The Swiss economy is pretty stable and given its neutral stance in politics, this pair tends to behave in an isolated manner without any noticeable correlations. Having said that, the Swiss authorities tend to forget they're a part of a global marketplace and have been known to spring nasty surprises that sometimes causes this pair to jump around wildly.

- NZDUSD - Called the kiwi, this pair is between the New Zealand Dollar and the U.S Dollar. The kiwi tracks the aussie quite closely but is slightly more volatile. Trading volumes are high mostly during the Asian session. There are good volumes in the New York session but this tapers off completely once New York closes.

The major pairs generally witness good volumes at all times and good liquidity levels throughout the day, even if their home markets aren't in session or if volumes aren't at their peak. Given the 24-hour nature of the market you will need to keep in mind that prices often reverse or completely contradict what happened earlier in the day.

It isn't uncommon to see the Asian currencies reverse their moves when New York opens and to then resume their original paths when Asia opens once again (Chen, 2020). Such behavior is just something the FX trader has to learn to deal with. Aside from these pairs, there are a number of pairs called the minors and these are greater in number.

- EURGBP - The euro and the british pound used to be a relatively unexciting pair but in recent time has received large doses of adrenaline. As of this current writing, this pair is all over the place and is experiencing huge volatility thanks to political situations in Europe and the U.K

- EURAUD - The Euro and the aussie dollar. This pair tracks the EURUSD quite closely and is more dependent on the behavior of the Euro than the Aussie.
- EURCAD - Trading this well requires you to keep up to speed with whatever the USDCAD is upto.
- EURCHF - This is a relatively stable pair and tracks the USDCHF closely. Generally, this pair is slightly more volatile.
- EURNZD - This pair tracks the EURAUD closely and is slightly more volatile.
- GBPJPY - This is one of the more interesting currency pairs. It follows the USDJPY closely but has been known to break away and do its own thing of late, thanks to Brexit.
- GBPAUD - This pair mimics the GBPUSD but also has significant input from whatever the AUDUSD is doing. Generally the Asian session sees it mimic the latter while the european session sees it mimic the former.
- GBPCAD - This pair is particularly volatile and mimics the USDCAD.
- GBPCHF - This pair follows the USDCHF closely but as with all GBP pairs, it is on the volatile side.

- GBPNZD - This behaves in the same way as the GBPAUD does but with greater degrees of volatility.
- AUDCAD - This pair witnesses good volumes mostly during the American session despite the presence of the AUD. Both currencies are heavily dependent on commodity prices so you should look out for those when trading this pair.
- AUDJPY - A stalwart of the Asian session. This pair witnesses huge volumes when Asia is open and then completely dies out for the rest of the day. Despite this, it is a safe pair to trade when it is active.
- AUDNZD - This pair witnesses a smaller window of activity when Asia is open. This is due to the fact that Sydney and Auckland close prior to Tokyo closing. Thus, by the time Europe opens, volume in this pair is quite low.
- CADJPY - This pair tracks the USDJPY quite closely.

There are a couple more minor pairs, but these aren't all that important. Generally speaking, minor pairs witness greater volatility across the board. This is partly because their volumes are far more dependent on the session that is currently live. While you can reasonably trade the majors throughout the day, you ideally want to be trading the minors when their home markets are open.

The final category of FX instruments is termed the exotics. As the name suggests this is pretty much every other currency pair in the world you can think of outside of the ones already listed. For example, the USDINR is an exotic pair and represents the exchange rate between the U.S Dollar and Indian Rupee. In case you're wondering where China fits into all of this, you must know that China does not allow its currency to freely float on the market.

In other words, the Chinese government fixes the exchange rate to the USD and that is that. There are many countries that do this to their currencies, but China is easily the biggest and most noteworthy of economies that does this.

Exotic pairs see extreme volatility as well as low levels of liquidity. In other words, there aren't many traders operating in it and when you do manage to get a trade through, you'll see huge swings in prices. While high volatility is a good thing, it is helpful only when it is paired with good liquidity.

Volatility that is caused by illiquidity is a bad thing. What does this mean? Let's say you wish to sell a pen in the open market. For whatever reason you find a buyer that is willing to pay you $5 for it, two buyers at $20 and that's it. There are no more buyers. Being a motivated seller, you'll obviously sell it for $20. Thus, the price of the pen moved from $3 (assuming this was what you bought it for) all the way to $20 thanks to illiquidity.

A fact of trading is that you never want to be isolated or going against the crowd. When this happens, you'll be faced with a highly illiquid market and you're not going to be able to do what you want. As a beginner, it is important that you remember this. Look to join the crowd in whichever direction it is pushing the market in. Don't try to be one of those heroes who tries to call market bottoms or market tops and ends up losing his shirt.

Pips

Another aspect of FX pairs you must know is that they don't move in units of dollars and cents. After all, how could a EURAUD pair move in denominations of US dollars? Typically, FX pair prices are represented as a number followed by four or five decimals such as X.XXXX(X).

In this denomination the fourth number after the decimal represents the smallest possible move in the pair. This move is called a pip. For example, if the price of EURUSD is 1.2345 and if it moves to 1.2346, it has moved by one pip. If the price moves from 1.2345 to 1.2355, the price has moved 10 pips and so on.

The only exception are the JPY pairs where the prices are XXX.XX(X). Here the second number after the decimal represents the smallest possible move in price. For example, if the USDJPY moves from 123.45 to

123.47, this is a two pip move. If it moves from 123.45 to 123.65, this is a 20 pip move.

Derivatives

Just as with the stock market, the forex market has its own share of derivatives. Generally speaking, you don't need to worry about the large majority of these. There is one type of instrument you should be aware of though and these are contracts for difference or CFDs.

A CFD is an instrument that you'll find only with forex brokers. These instruments mimic the movement of any other stock or stock index around the world. You can also trade CFDs on commodities such as gold, oil, silver and so on. This is how they're structured.

If you wish to place a trade on oil contracts, you will have to sign up for an account with a broker that gives you access to oil futures (futures are a derivative). Doing all this is a pain because you'll need to satisfy residency requirements as well as file a ton of paperwork.

Instead of going through all of this your forex broker creates a contract that reflects the price movement of the oil futures contract. They do this by entering into an agreement with the interbank dealer they've signed up with. As a trader you simply buy or sell the CFD as if it were a regular instrument and earn a profit or loss based on your trade.

As long as you manage your risk wisely, there is no danger when it comes to trading CFDs. The leverage you can access when trading them is the same as what you'll have when trading FX instruments. The only downside to a CFD is that you might find yourself in a position where the broker is trading against you.

This will be made clear in the next chapter where we'll deal with the specifics of how brokers work.

Chapter 2:

Brokers

The forex broker is a very different beast from the one you'll find in the stock market. A big reason for this has to do with the way the market is structured. Leverage is essential in forex to make money but is only optional in the stock market. Due to this, forex brokers tend to have strong risk management systems that might cause you a few problems when you trade.

Then there's the fact that all of that leverage places the broker in a situation where they're in a conflict of interest with regard to their clients. However, I'm running ahead of myself. Let's first understand what leverage is.

Making Money in Forex

You've already learned how when trading forex, you're actually trading the difference in exchange rates between currencies. The thing about exchange rates is that they won't fluctuate very much over the course of a year, let alone a single day. Think about it: You're extremely unlikely to wake up and find that the Canadian dollar is now worth half as much as it was worth yesterday.

In other words, if the exchange rate yesterday was 1.345, it's highly unlikely that this rate is going to change to 2.695 overnight! If this happened all forms of trade would collapse. In fact, economies that experience this kind of inflation in their currencies do tend to collapse since people cannot afford to live in such situations.

Thus, currency exchange rates move very little, often less than a cent, during the course of a day and they do this thanks to the way the macroeconomic picture works. Central banks in various countries around the world keep a close eye on interest rates and governments introduce economic policies to ensure stability. All of these actions impact that country's currency and as a result, exchange rates remain stable.

This isn't great news from a trading perspective. If something doesn't move, how are you going to make money from it? This is where leverage helps and is why it's essential to make money in forex.

Margin and Leverage

Consider a hypothetical scenario: You have the chance to invest in a financial instrument that costs $100. You're certain it's going to go up to $110. The problem is that you have just $1 in your pocket. You approach a friend or a lender and convince them to lend you $99 and promise to pay them interest of 5% on the loan. In other words, you promise to pay them a round $5 for this loan.

Using their money and your $1, you buy the instrument for $100 and your prediction turns out to be right. The price does increase to $110 and you sell it for a profit of $10. From that $10, you pay the lender their $5 and they're happy as well. You pocket the remaining $5 as profit.

What do the numbers look like in this scenario? You invested just $1 of your own cash but earned a profit of $5 which is a 400% gain! You earned this astronomical amount despite the fact that the overall price moved just 10% (from 100 to 110.) You could do this because you leveraged your investment.

Leverage refers to the degree to which you've borrowed money to finance your investment. In this case, your leverage is 1:99. For every dollar of your own you invested, you borrowed $99. This allowed you to translate a 10% move in price to a personal gain of 400%. That's the power of leverage in a nutshell.

It goes both ways though. Let's say the price of the instrument declined from $100 to $95. Your loss is $5 on this position (a position is simply a trade that you place in the market.) You close this position for a $5 loss. What do the numbers look like now?

First off, you owe $5 to the lender. Next, you've lost $5 on the trade. This brings your total loss to $10. given that you've invested $1 on this trade, that is a personal loss of 1000%! You've lost this amount despite the instrument declining by just 5% (from 100 to 95.) In other words, you've lost more than what you invested.

This is why leverage needs to be managed extremely carefully. In the forex market, price moves are extremely small and thus you need leverage to be able to make any amount of decent money. The problem is that most beginner traders lose their heads and opt for extremely high levels of leverage.

In the United States, a trader can access up to 1:50 leverage. In other words, you can borrow $50 for every dollar you invest. Internationally, the leverage rates are far higher. 1:100 is a common leverage rate with some brokers even offering 1:500. This is why risk management is so important in forex and is why I mentioned earlier that it's easy to make money in forex but keeping it is another issue entirely.

Let's look at how placing trades in forex works.

Lots

When you sign up for a brokerage account with a forex broker, you're going to see that order placement is different from what it is in the stock market. While stocks are usually bought in numbers (five shares or 10 shares etc.) forex instruments are bought in lots. There are three types of lots in forex trading instruments:

1. Standard
2. Mini
3. Micro

A standard lot is 100,000 of the base currency in the pair. For example, if you buy one standard lot of EURUSD you're buying 100,000 Euros and selling the equivalent amount of USD. This sounds like a lot but remember that you have access to 1:50 leverage at the very least. Thus, in order to buy these many Euros, you need to invest a little over $2,000 with your broker.

A mini-lot is 10,000 of the base currency and a micro-lot is 1,000 of it. Some brokers even offer a nano-lot which is 100 units of the base currency. The majority of brokers quote the number of lots following a x.xx convention.

For example, if you buy 1.20 EURUSD, you're buying one standard lot and 20 mini-lots of EURUSD. Some brokers break it out into full numbers. So instead of displaying your position size as 1.20 they'll display it as 120,000.

Pip Values

Now that you know what a lot is and what a pip is it's time to look at how you can calculate profit and loss numbers on your position. In stocks, this is pretty straightforward. You subtract the selling price from the buy price and multiply that by the number of shares bought and this gives you your profit or loss. In forex, you're dealing with multiple currencies, so it isn't as straightforward.

Let's take the example of the USDCAD and let's assume the price is being quoted as 1.03. This means (as you learned in the previous chapter) one USD is worth 1.03 CAD. So how many USD is a one pip movement worth? We calculate this by using the formula below:

Pip value = one pip / price = 0.0001 / 1.03 = 0.000097

The 'one pip' component of the formula is simply the smallest movement in that currency pair. If we were to buy one standard lot of USDCAD, one pip's movement in this position would be worth:

Position pip value = position size * pip value = 100000*.000097 = $9.70

Thus, if the price of this pair moves from 1.03 to 1.0301, you've just made yourself $9.70 on this position.

The calculation is the same in non-USD pairs. However, in order to translate the value back into USD, you will need to multiply or divide that result by the exchange rate between the currency in question and USD.

Let's say the GBPJPY was trading at 123.01. The pip value in this case will be 0.000081 GBP. If you bought a standard lot, this gives us a position pip value of 8.10 GBP per pip. To translate this to USD you will need to multiply this value by the price of the GBPUSD currency pair.

We multiply here because the pair represents the value of one GBP in USD. If the price is 1.55, this means one GBP is worth 1.55 USD. Thus 8.1 GBP is worth (8.1*1.5) $12.15 per pip.

You need to know the position value per pip because this is how you'll be able to calculate the amount of money you're risking on the trade. When you place a trade you'll be placing two orders. The first is the order to buy or sell the instrument at a particular price.

The second order will be your stop loss. This order is placed at a level where you will exit the trade for your maximum loss if prices move against you. When placing a trade you should first fix your maximum loss amount on the trade, then your entry price, then your stop loss price and only then should you figure out how many units of the instrument you will need to buy.

To do this you will divide the maximum loss amount by the distance between the buy and sell price. Next, divide this number by a single pip (the smallest movement in the pair which is either 0.0001 or 0.01). Multiply this by the stop loss price to arrive at the position size.

All of this is complicated. Markets move quickly and you will need to calculate your position sizes quickly in order to enter and exit. Thankfully, there are a number of calculators available online that you can use. You don't need to worry about creating a spreadsheet or calculator to help you do any of this.

A good one is available at https://www.babypips.com/tools/position-size-calculator. Simply enter your account currency, your account balance, your risk percentage (the percent of your account you're risking on the trade), your stop loss size in pips (the difference between your entry and stop loss price) and choose the currency pair you're trading.

This will give you your position size both in units as well as break it down by lots. For example, if you see a breakdown such as 10 standard lots, 100 mini-lots and 1000 micro- lots, your position size is 1.11 or 1,11,000 units.

Now that all of this is out of the way, let's look at the state of broker regulation in the forex industry.

Broker Regulation

As I mentioned earlier, the forex broker world can seem like the Wild West upon first impression. The truth is that in the United States many of the unethical and illegal practices that used to be prevalent have been banished and are now subject to strict regulatory scrutiny.

U.S brokers are subject to regulation by the Commodity and Futures Trading Commission or CFTC and the National Futures Association or NFA. In addition to this the Securities and Exchange Commission (SEC) and Financial Regulatory Authority (FINRA) also have oversight in this space. A lot of the duties of these bodies overlap and between them, forex brokers are a well-regulated bunch.

In the United States, you can access a maximum leverage of 1:50 without exception. In addition to this, U.S brokers are not allowed to practice what is called 'B' booking which I'll explain shortly. Brokers will require standard documentation from you when opening an account such as your proof of residence via a utility bill or bank statement, your social security number etc. Crucially, forex trading does not suffer from the PDT regulation.

Pattern Day Trading or PDT is something that many stock market traders have to contend with. PDT states that if a trader places four or more trades within the span of a work week, they will need to have at least $25,000 as margin (account balance) in their accounts.

This means that in order to successfully day trade in the U.S, you will need to have at least $25,000 as capital. This rule does not apply to forex. You will need to possess the broker stipulated minimums in your account and that's it. These range from $500 to $5,000.

There are different types of brokers you can choose from so let's take a look at these now.

Straight Through Processing

STP brokers typically sign up with a number of different interbank dealers and route their clients' orders directly to those dealers. The interbank dealers are referred to as liquidity providers or LPs by the broker. STP brokers also usually do not have dealing desks of their own.

In other words, an STP broker will typically not take the other side of your trade since they will likely not have any traders of their own. They simply charge you a commission and pass your trade onto their LPs and have it executed. Keep in mind that it is possible for an STP broker to have dealing desks and that an STP broker can choose to signup with just one LP instead of multiple ones.

This depends on the individual broker so make sure to carry out your research with regard to this point.

Electronic Communication Network

ECN brokers function a lot like STPs but with a few differences. For one thing they do not have contracts with just a few LPs but rather are part of a network of dealers themselves. These brokers will send your order to the ECN order pool where it will be matched with a larger pool of orders as compared to an STP.

These brokers are typically larger in size and might charge you higher commissions. They also might have their own dealing desks. Once again, it's important to conduct your research when choosing one of these companies to open an account with.

Dealing Versus Non Dealing

Another classification that can be applied to brokers are whether they're dealers or non dealers. Typically, STP brokers will be non dealers and won't have dealing desks. Dealing desks pose both reward and risk to forex brokers. By having desks, the broker has the opportunity to make a market in a particular instrument.

What I mean by making a market is that they have the opportunity to sell you an instrument at a slightly higher price than what is available for in the market. This sort of behavior is illegal in the stock market but is permitted in the forex market for some reason.

These brokers often market themselves as being 'zero commission' brokers. In other words they don't need to charge you a commission since they're taking the other side of the trade from you and are selling you instruments at slightly marked up prices. This practice is often termed 'B' booking.

Every dealing desk broker has two sets of order books: The A book and the B book. The A book orders are sent directly to the LP or the ECN while the B book orders are sold at a marked up price to the broker's clients. The A book's orders are charged a commission while the B book's orders are charged zero commissions but the prices are slightly inflated.

A term that is used to signify B booking is to call it spread inflation. Your broker might also tell you that they adjust their commissions into the spread. This is simply them telling you that they're B booking your orders and are taking the other side of your position. If you happen to lose, they win and make money.

I must mention that not all dealing desk brokers practice B booking. In the United States, B booking is technically legal in forex despite it being illegal in stocks. However, there aren't many brokers that practice this. The best way to figure out if a broker is a B booker is to simply ask them about it. They have no reason to hide it since it's legal and will disclose it to you.

In the international markets, the best way to spot a B booker is to look at their commission structures and their domiciles. If they're based out of a tax haven such as the British Virgin Islands or Cyprus or Belize, you can bet your bottom dollar that they're B bookers. In fact, such brokers are probably a bunch of traders sitting around trading against you instead of actually performing the tasks a broker should.

The bottom line for you to understand with all of this is: Pick a broker who is based out of a fully regulated jurisdiction. Choose an STP broker as much as possible since this will give you the best possible set of circumstances in which you can succeed. There is one last factor you should take into account when choosing a broker.

Risk

The fact of the matter is that the forex markets are extremely risky. The high rates of leverage offered expose not just traders but also brokers to undue risks. After all, they're the ones lending you the money. If you manage to lose money in far greater multiples of your account balance, guess who foots the bill? Obviously, if you're the one who loses the money, you'll be the first person the creditor calls but if you cannot pay the money back, the broker is the one who is liable for some percentage of that amount.

Also consider that if your losses are huge, you cannot make the broker whole either. While you lose $1, they lose the $99 that they've lent you. The forex markets are governed by a wide variety of factors. Cross border political factors, the prices of commodities, government regulation changes, central bank announcements, all of these play a crucial role in how currencies move.

A broker has to have robust risk management protocols to ensure they aren't over exposed to any particular risk.

It is impossible for you to evaluate this, but one tell-tale sign is to monitor how the broker keeps tabs on margin requirements as world events unfold.

Margin refers to the total value of your account balance. It includes cash plus the value of any open positions you have in there. When risks increase, your broker will typically increase the margin requirements for the instruments that are affected. For example, when the Brexit vote was taking place, many reliable brokers decreased the amount of leverage they offered clients and called for clients to post more margin in their accounts to reduce risk.

In addition to this some brokers suspended trading for short periods to avoid exposing themselves and their clients to huge and unpredictable price movements. Another tell- tale sign is to look at the quality of the LPs the broker has signed up with. Are all the LPs concentrated in one place or are they diversified?

For example, a broker that has signed up with LPs solely in Australia is exposing themselves to undue risk with regard to whatever happens to that country's economy. The sole exception to this are American brokers who often are legally bound to sign up with American banks thanks to disclosure requirements.

Assess the quality of the LPs in terms of reputation and you'll get a good feel for the risk management that they practice.

Spreads

A common sticking point for a lot of beginner traders in the markets is the concept of the price spread. They often switch on financial news channels and see that everything seems to have just one price associated with it. This is not the case in either FX or the stock market.

When you place a trade in the market you will see that there is a price you have to pay if you wish to buy the instrument and another price you receive if you wish to sell it. These prices are separated by a few pips in most cases. This difference in prices is called the spread.

The lower the spread is, the more tradable the instrument is since it indicates that a large number of traders are active in it. This situation is referred to as an instrument being liquid (as opposed to illiquid.) During times of volatility, price spreads increase massively. Volatility is when an instrument begins to jump around all over the place forcefully.

An instrument such as the EURUSD that moves mostly sideways is referred to as being nonvolatile. However, when an announcement happens (either with regards to interest rates or politics) the pair starts moving around all over the place. In short, it becomes volatile.

Volatility for the trader is a lot like leverage. It can cut both ways. On one hand, volatility ensures that prices move in a given direction with a lot of force. However, prices are equally liable to move in the other direction, hit your stop loss and then swing in the opposite direction.

Managing volatility is a part of good risk management and you'll learn all about this later in this book as well as in the next one in this series which deals with advanced techniques. We've entered the world of price movements with this section and it's only logical that we now take the time to look at how price charts can be interpreted.

Chapter 3:

The Price Chart

The amount of profit and loss that you earn from your trades depends on the degree with which price changes. Traders often use a whole bunch of technical analysis indicators to help them figure out what price is going to do next. Before we look at indicators though, it is important for you to understand the price chart itself and how it can be used to provide you with signals ahead of time.

This chapter is going to introduce you to the world of candlesticks and the price patterns that they form. If you're already familiar with candlesticks, you can skip the first portions of this chapter where I talk about what they are. However, I urge you to take a look at the patterns because there are some important lessons there that you will not find anywhere else.

Candles and Bars

The problem of representing price movements accurately on a chart has always plagued traders. Keep in mind that trading in stocks and financial instruments has been around since the mid 1600's. Back then traders had to draw charts by hand to help them figure out which way prices were likely to move.

Forex trading is a relatively new phenomenon when looked at in this regard. Despite the size of the forex market dwarfing the combined value of all of the stock markets in the world many times over, forex trading has been around only since the 1970's when most countries in the world decided to move away from the gold standard.

I'm not going to bore you with a history lesson here. My point is that price charting techniques borrow a lot from their stock market counterparts because stock markets have been around for so much longer. One of the ways that American traders traditionally employed was to use price bars to represent movements.

When you switch on CNBC the charts you see on there are line charts. They look something like what you see in Figure 1.

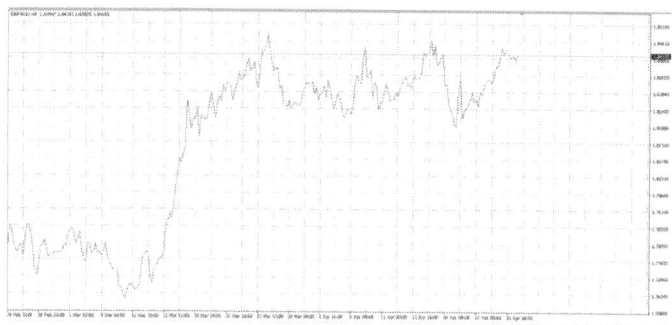

Figure 1 : Line Chart

There are some elements of the chart that I need to clarify. First off, this is a chart of the GBPAUD and it is an H4 chart. H4 refers to the time frame that is relevant here. You'll learn about time frames shortly. On the right hand side, you can see the prices listed and on the bottom you can see the date.

It is possible to get a good idea of the long term movement in price via a line chart. However, it isn't of much use for traders because of the information it leaves out (Chen, 2020). A line chart is constructed in the following manner. Let's say you wish to plot price movements on a daily basis. You look at what price the instrument closed at yesterday and place a dot on a chart.

You look at what it closed the day before yesterday and place another dot and so on for as long as you wish. You then connect these dots with a line and a curve forms. This is how a daily line chart is constructed. In other words, the time frame here is daily. You can choose different time frames to represent price moves.

Here are the most commonly used time frames in trading:

- Weekly
- Daily
- Four hour/ H4
- One hour/ H1
- 30 minute/M30

- 15 minute/M15
- Five minute/M5
- One minute/M1

You would construct a daily chat by joining all of the prices that instrument ended up at the end of each day to form a curve. An H4 chart is created by doing the same thing every four hours. Similarly, an M30 chart is created by joining the prices together to form a line at the end of every 30 minutes.

Let's say you're creating an H4 line chart like the one in Figure 1 for the GBPAUD. To create one you simply check in at the end of every four hours and place a dot on the chart and extend the curve. The issue with doing this, from an information standpoint, is that prices are never static.

They keep moving around. Let's say the price of GBPAUD moves from 1.8419 to 1.9345, goes down to 1.8345 and then moves back up to 1.8419 as the four hour window closes. You would simply mark another dot at 1.8419 and extend the line from the previous dot horizontally.

The impression given by the line chart is that prices were stable since the line will be perfectly horizontal. However, the line chart doesn't mention that prices were extremely volatile. price moved by close to 1,000 pips up, moved down by another 1,100 pips and only then moved back to their original levels! Clearly, something better is needed to capture these price moves on a chart.

Bar charts were created to capture these moves but the best way of depicting such price moves is to look at candlestick charts. These are a Japanese creation and are easily the best way of depicting price action.

Structure

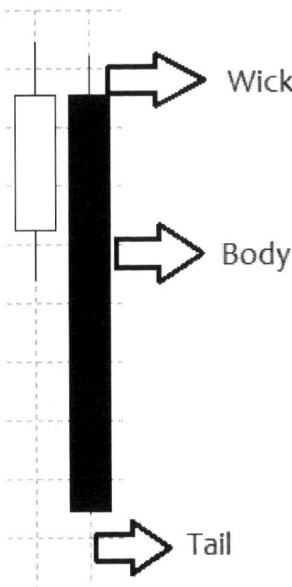

Figure 2: Candlestick Structure

Figure 2 illustrates two candlesticks or candles as they're called. For ease of communication I'm going to use the words candle and bars interchangeably in the rest of this book. There are three portions to a candle as you can see:

1. The body
2. The wick
3. The tail

The body has a couple of attributes that you must pay special attention to. The first of these is the color and the second is the size. In Figure 2, the second candle's body is much larger than the first. It is also colored black as opposed to white as is the case with the first candle.

These candles have been taken from an H4 chart. One candle represents four hours' worth of price movements. As you can imagine, prices aren't standing still and will jump up and down all the time. In fact, they can open the four hour period at a certain price and then close the period above the opening level, below it or at the same price.

If the open happens to be greater than the close, the bar is referred to as being bearish. This is because price declined and all price declines in the markets are referred to as being bearish. If the close happens to be greater than the open, this is a bullish bar. Price increases of all kinds are referred to as being bullish.

Don't be tempted into thinking that bullish bars are somehow better than bearish ones. This is a classic rookie mistake. It is possible to make money off both types of price movements. In fact, you should not hesitate to 'short' any instrument in order to make money. Shorting is when you sell an instrument prior to buying it back later. This is opposed to going 'long' where you buy first and then sell.

Long and short aside, the color of the candle immediately lets you know whether the price movement is bullish or bearish. A dark colored body indicates bearishness while a white colored body indicates bullishness. Remember that with bullish bars the open is lesser than the close while with bearish bars the close is lesser than the open.

Thus, in Figure 2, the bottom of the second, bearish candlestick's body is its close while the top of its body is its open. The opposite is the case with the first, bullish candlestick. Next, we'll take a look at the wicks and tails. As price moves, it hits a certain level that becomes the highest point it reaches during that time interval. This level is called the high.

Similarly, it reaches a low as well. The highest point of the wick indicates the high and the lowest point of the tail indicates the low. In Figure 2, the second bar doesn't have any noticeable tail. This is because the close happens to be the low. Similarly, it is possible for the high to be equal to the open and for a bar to not have any wick.

Candlesticks in a short picture manage to convey a wealth of information about price movement during intervals as you can see. Contrast this to a line chart where all you get to see is the close. Why is the information about the high and the low and bullishness or bearishness so important?

The fact is that this is a direct insight into the way traders currently feel about prices. Candlesticks form a number of patterns that can inform us about the way in which prices are likely to move. Let's look at some of these to see how we can draw such conclusions.

Price Patterns

In this book I'll be introducing three powerful price patterns that you can make use of to start interpreting price moves right now. There are a large number of candlestick patterns you can use but a lot of these are best used by more advanced traders who have a better idea of how markets work.

The reason I'm introducing just three simple ones is that these can be traded in pretty much any market, no matter what it is doing. In order to apply candlestick patterns properly, you will need to match the pattern with appropriate trading conditions. Mny traders approach this topic as they would a geometry test.

They think it's a question of finding the correct shape and then blindly doing what the shape tells them to do according to a formula. This is not how trading works. If it were that simple, everyone would be a brilliant trader. As you study these patterns, keep the underlying order flow characteristics in mind. I will be discussing these in great detail, so take the time to understand not just what the pattern is but why it is powerful.

As long as you understand the why behind the shape, the shape itself is immaterial. You will begin to see patterns everywhere since you won't be restricted to trading ust a few shapes that every single trader out there is already looking at.

Pin Bars

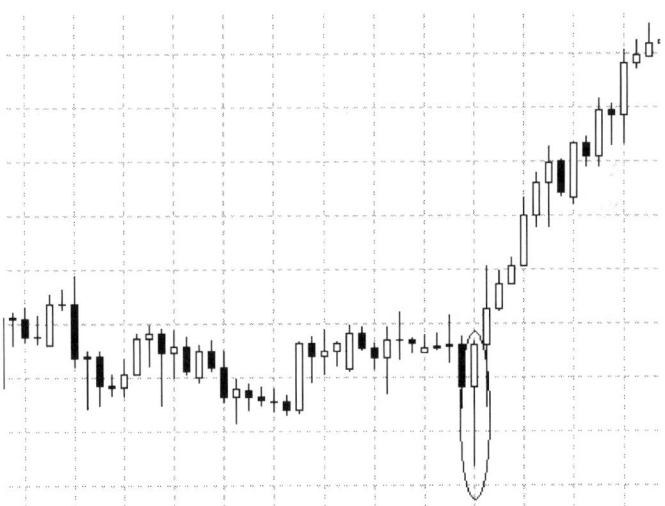

Figure 3: Pin Bar

The pin bar is one of the most versatile and powerful price patterns you can trade. The bar within the circle in

Figure 3 indicates a pin bar. This particular pin bar has a body that is smaller in size when compared to its tail. Pin bars that have long tails are bullish indicators.

Pin bars can have long wicks as well and these are bearish in nature. Bullish and bearish in this context means that price is either going to go up or go down once these price patterns form. Pin bars can be used as both continuation patterns as well as reversal patterns. So what do these mean?

A continuation pattern is one that indicates that prices are likely going to continue in the direction they've been headed in. From Figure 3, we see that prices have been moving sideways prior to the pin bar. Once the bullish pin is formed, this is an indication that prices will now start moving up. Sideways movements are often formed when prices take a breather from moving up or down for a long time.

So what do pin bars communicate to us in terms of the underlying order flow? Let's examine the pin in Figure 3 to learn more about this. First off, we have the relatively small body. The body happens to be bullish but this really isn't all that important. You can have a pin bar that signals bullishness be bearish in color and vice versa. The important thing to focus on is the size of the body and not its color.

The size of the body generally needs to be less than ½ the size of the tail or the wick. Some traders require a 3x multiple when comparing the size of the tail or wick with the body. What does the large tail in Figure 3 convey to us. It tells us that the bears tried pushing prices down to the low and at that point were repelled by the bulls in the market.

The bulls managed to push prices well away from the low and in fact got prices to close near the high of that interval. This is a clear sign of bullish strength. After all, only a strong bullish push can negate bearishness to this extent. This is an indication that the bulls are ready to push prices even higher and this is precisely what happens.

Similarly, if you spot a pin bar with a large wick and small body, it means that the bears managed to push bulls back and pushed prices down from the highs. When it comes to pin bars, you want to see the body of the candle be as close to the top as possible. A bar where the body lies in the middle and where the tail and wick are equal in size is not a genuine pin bar.

From an order flow perspective, let's reason why this is. A bar that has an equally large tail and wick indicates that the bears and bulls exerted equal and opposite pressure on prices and couldn't win out over the other side. As a result prices closed somewhere in the middle, close to where they opened.

The general theme you want to look for in a pin bar is one of dominance. There shouldn't be any doubt when looking at the bar that one side of the market won out over the other. A word of caution at this point. As powerful as pin bars are, you don't want to go around taking every single one you find. Figure 4 illustrates the danger of doing this.

Figure 4: Bullish and Bearish Pin Bars

In Figure 4 we have instances of both bullish and bearish pin bars. The bars within the circles are bullish whereas the ones within the rectangles are bearish. The average unsuccessful trader's approach to this chart would be to blindly follow all of these signals. They would enter short twice and go long thrice.

Clearly, this is not the intelligent thing to do. Instead, what you need to do is to take a step back and survey the overall market conditions. While the pin bar is a powerful price action indicator, at the end of the day it is just one bar. Its presence does not negate the effects of all the price bars that came before it.

In Figure 4, we see that the first two bearish pins are preceded by extremely bearish bars. Clearly, the price is going down. Thus, heeding the call of the two bearish bars is the right thing to do. As prices decrease, we see that the bullish pins are formed. There has been zero indication that prices are going to turn and reverse upwards. Just because one bar with the shape of a pin has been formed, this doesn't mean all of the bearish bars that came before it have been invalidated.

The smart thing to do here is ignore those bullish pins and continue to look for bearish pins. This is because the overall market is headed that way. My point in illustrating this example is that the pin bar is something that reveals price action. It is not the cause of it. A bullish pin is not going to automatically guarantee bullishness just because it has been formed.

The same applies for a bearish pin that forms in a bullish environment. Do not automatically enter trades just because you spot a pin. Evaluate which way the market is headed and then enter. If you spot pins in large sideways movements, you can safely trade both sides of the market. That is, you can go long and short as the situation may warrant.

However, in short sideways movements or in clear directional moves as in Figure 4, go with the direction in which the market is headed and don't try to trade against the trend. I had mentioned in the beginning of this section that pins can be used as both continuation as well as reversal signals.

Using pins to spot reversals is a profitable technique but it is one that is best left for more advanced traders. This is because you need to understand order flow much better to be able to spot valid signals. Given that spotting such conditions requires skill and experience, beginner traders are best served using pins as continuation signals.

As a final word on pins, don't get hung up too much on the exact ratio between the body and the tail or wick. What's important is that the bar itself clearly signifies that one side of the market managed to overpower the other decisively. Another aspect of pins you should watch out for is the size of the bar itself.

I'm not talking about the size of the body but the overall size of the bar from wick to tail. The larger it is, the greater is the price action implication. Look to take pins that are at least as large as the bars that surround it. If the pin happens to be too small, then it is unlikely that price will follow what it implies.

Two Bar Reversals

The two bar reversal pattern can be seen as a continuation of the pin bar signal. What I mean is that this pattern can be viewed as a deconstructed pin bar. When you combine the two bars within this pattern, you will find that the result is a pin bar shape that is a powerful predictor of which way price is most likely to go.

Figure 5 displays this pattern.

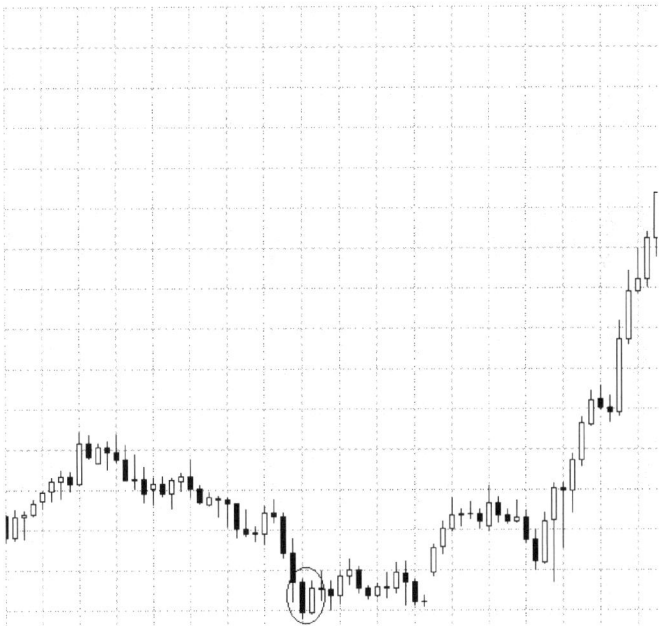

Figure 5: Two Bar Reversal

The two bar reversal is a pattern that consists of two bars with the second being an almost exact opposite of the first. In the case of Figure 5, we have a bullish two bar reversal with the second bar bullish and the first bar bearish. The second bar is almost of the exact same size as the first. In other words, whatever happened with the first bar is negated by the second.

If you were to superimpose the second bar over the first and create a new bar, you will see that a pin is formed. In other words, we use the open of the first bar and the close of the second, with the low and high of the first. Since price closes right back up near the open in this case, we'll have a pin bar with a bearish body but one that provides a pretty strong bullish signal.

From a price action or order flow perspective, the implications are straightforward to understand. In Figure 5 we have prices moving sideways (not shown in the figure) after a long bull trend and given what the environment looks like, we're simply looking for some form of confirmation that prices are ready to go back up.

This arrives in the form of the two bar reversal and price eventually moves up. Notice that as price starts to move up, we see a strong bullish pin bar. This could have been an entry point as well but the two bar reversal prints much before this.

The bearish version of this signal would be when the first bar is bullish and the second is bearish. In this case, the combination of the two bars would be a bar with a significant wick and that is a bearish indication. As with the pin, this signal is a powerful continuation and reversal signal.

However, beginner traders are best served by trading this as a continuation pattern and not worrying about using this to spot the end of trends or anything fancy like that. As is the case with pins, you are likely to spot multiple signals in a cluster of bars that will indicate both bullishness and bearishness.

The thing to do is to align yourself in the direction that the market is already headed in and pay heed to only those signals that line up with the direction you wish to trade in. A common mistake that traders make with two bar reversals is to simply look at the bodies of the candles and not pay attention to the wicks and tails.

In other words, you can have two candles whose bodies are exact opposites of one another, but the wicks and tails cause the combination of both bars to look nothing like a pin. Figure 6 is an example of this.

Figure 6: An Invalid Two Bar Reversal

The invalid signal is indicated by a circle. These two bars occur in a sideways movement that is quite lengthy. In such conditions, going both long and short is a valid move. With the two bars highlighted, you can see how the bearish bar completely negates whatever the bullish bar did and closes lower than the open of the bullish bar.

If you were to superimpose just the bodies of these candles upon one another, a pin bar would be the result. However, notice the tail on the second bar. The actual composite bar of these two would contain the open of the first bar, the close of the second, the high of the first and the low of the second. The result is a bar that has an almost equal sized wick and a tail with the body somewhere near the middle of the bar.

In other words, this isn't a pin but is actually a bar that is indicating indecisiveness on the market's part. As such you should stay away from this one since it doesn't really indicate anything.

Engulfers

Engulfers or engulfing bars as they're sometimes referred to are perhaps the easiest signals to spot in the market. This is because they're just obvious and large on a price chart. Figure 7 shows what I'm talking about.

Figure 7: Bullish Engulfing Bar

In this figure, the engulfing bar is the final bullish bar in the box. Notice how it dwarfs and engulfs pretty much every single bar that comes before it. It is the most dominant bar on this chart and as far as a price action signal goes, it doesn't get any clearer than this!

While the previous two price action signals were meant to be traded as continuation signals, the engulfer is an example of a reversal pattern. This is because it often occurs near the end of a trend. While this is not highlighted, the price environment in Figure 7 is one where a bearish trend is coming to an end and price is moving sideways with no particular momentum.

The existence of this huge engulfing bar leaves no doubt as to which way prices are going to go next. Notice that price doesn't immediately take off upwards. It moves up, falls back down well into the territory of the engulfer and only then moves up. With bullish moves this is usually the case.

When you spot a bullish engulfer like in Figure 8, you can wait for a while for the price to pull back down for you to enter at a better price level. when it comes to bearish engulfers though, this is not always the case. Bear trends behave differently from bull trends and you will find that prices will drop immediately once the pattern makes itself known.

From a price action perspective, it's pretty simple to figure out what's going on here. The bulls (with reference to Figure 7) have had enough and are looking to push prices back up. They test the market out by pushing prices up and encounter almost no resistance. This is indicated by the huge body of the engulfing bar.

The previous bars and order flow are literally swallowed up. However, before pushing prices too far up, they take the time to mop up any of the remaining bearish presence in the market. This explains why prices dip lower before shooting up. Bullish trends tend to see greater levels of trader participation than bearish ones.

This is why prices will often struggle a bit before finally shooting up since there are a larger number of traders trying to get good prices before allowing them to rise without any resistance. This is also why bull trends will last longer than bearish ones. Bear trends on the other hand are much sharper and attract a smaller crowd. They're quicker to manifest and end.

This doesn't mean that bear trends will form over the course of a single bar or that the market can turn on a dime and go down. What I mean is that the trend reversal process prior to a bear trend is smaller in size than it is before a bull trend. As a beginner you don't need to worry about these reversal processes. Simply look for the appropriate price action pattern to help you spot when the process is complete and when the price is ready to move in a given direction.

One of the problems with price action patterns you might have noticed is that they tend to form all over the place and deciding which ones are valid and which ones are invalid can be a bit tricky. You could look at the market environment and this will give you a huge clue as to which direction you need to be trading in.

There is an additional technique that will help you figure this out. When combined together you will likely have no problems deciding which pattern is valid and which one needs to be ignored.

Chapter 4:

Support and Resistance

Those who have prior trading knowledge and experience will think they know all about support and resistance and will be tempted to skip this chapter. Again, I urge you to read it fully since you're likely to learn things you do not know as yet. For the complete beginners, support and resistance is an important concept that will help you make far more sense of the way the market is structured.

Let's begin by defining what they are.

Support and Resistance

When you look at a live price chart you will see that it is constantly moving. This is because there are numerous traders present in the market who are placing orders to buy or sell that particular instrument. If the number of sell orders are greater than buy orders, prices decline. If the buy orders are greater in number than sell orders, prices rise.

As prices move, you will also notice that it tends to return to certain areas on the chart and bounce off them. Often, these areas last for a long time and price repeatedly uses them as a springboard to move higher or lower. These levels are powerful because they represent areas where traders congregate. They congregate there because they agree over how price needs to move once it reaches that level.

These levels or zones are called support and resistance. A zone that results in prices bouncing upwards from it is called support. This is where the bulls come together to push prices upwards en masse. Zones that result in prices turning downwards from them are called resistance. This is where bears congregate and push prices down together.

When it comes to trading, there is no doubt that there is strength in numbers. If you recall from earlier in this book, I had mentioned how your job as a trader is to simply follow what the majority of traders in the market are doing. It is not to try and be the first to predict the new course of price. Support and resistance zones form naturally because smart traders are always looking for places where the greatest numbers of like minded traders reside.

Support and resistance is also where you must enter your trades from, for the most part. Whether you're using an indicator or using just candlestick patterns that you learned about in the previous chapter, entering from support or resistance will ensure the odds of success are in your favor.

This is because you're going to find a larger number of traders willing to back your trade in the direction you want it to go in. Support and resistance zones vary in terms of strength and the influence they exert on prices. Let's look at some of their characteristics and in the process learn more about them.

Swing Points

You are going to find many support and resistance zones in a price chart. This does not mean you should trade from each and every one of them. Instead, spot the strongest ones and look to place trades from there, according to what your entry signal dictates.

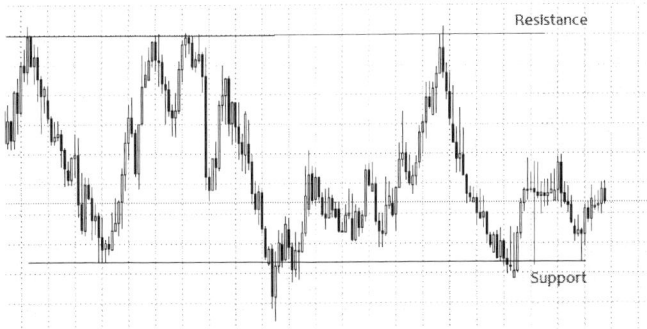

Figure 8: Support and Resistance

Figure 8 illustrates both support and resistance levels in a sideways price movement. Let's begin from the left of the chart and work our way forward. Price swings downwards quite forcefully as it reaches a certain level at the bottom and then swings right back up. Both of these swings, the downswing followed by the upswing give us a preliminary idea of where the support and resistance zones might lie.

Notice how strong the downswing is from the top and how the following upswing is just as strong. This indicates that whatever force was pushing prices down eventually met with an equal and opposite bullish force that pushed prices back up. As prices make their way back up, what could you surmise about what might happen next?

The most obvious conclusion you can form is that price might react downwards once more from the same area from where it initially swung down. After all, the traders that pushed price down originally are likely going to be present there this time as well. As price approaches this area once again, it hits it once, dips and then comes right back at it.

At this point, it forms a pin bar that is bearish in nature right at the resistance level. Price immediately swings back down. I'd like to point out that price does not swing down because of the pin bar. Rather the pin bar merely illuminates what is going on with the order flow.

As price makes its way back down what can we judge might happen from its past behavior? The support zone that exists near the prior swing low might exert itself once again, much like the resistance zone did on top. We could conceivably exit our short trades near this zone and seek to go long.

As it happens price crashes right through the level but then peeks back up above it. As it peeks back up, do you notice any price action pattern? There's a pin bar that is formed right at the support level. Price swings back up and eventually reaches the resistance zone where we can look to close our longs and go short again.

It helpfully prints a two bar reversal right at the resistance and price swings back down. As it swings down, there is a large pin bar that is formed but as of now, price hasn't followed through on it.

This little sequence illustrates how powerful combining price action patterns with support and resistance can be. The traders that are present at these zones/levels telegraph exactly what they're going to do thanks to the price action patterns and we're left in no doubt as to what will happen next (Chen, 2020).

Look to trade bullish patterns from support and bearish patterns from resistance. If you spot a bullish pattern at a resistance level, ignore it. Remember, the pattern itself is not as important as the underlying price action. Support and resistance indicate the nature of this in better ways than the patterns do.

Zones

From Figure 8 we can learn something very important about support and resistance levels. They aren't really levels as much as they're zones. Notice how the support zone seemingly gets violated when price approaches it the second time. Even the third time that price approaches it, it dips below the line that indicates the support level.

This is in contrast to the resistance where price seemingly hits the line right on the money before turning downwards. The fact is that the average support or resistance zone resembles the support zone in Figure 8 than the resistance in the same figure. This is because traders don't park themselves at exact levels in terms of prices.

They tend to cluster around a level. This happens because traders have different aims in the market. There are traders who are trading the M5 charts and those who are trading the weekly charts as well. The intervening time frames find a large number of traders operating in them as well.

It is unrealistic to expect all traders across all time frames to agree on the exact level at which price out to stop and turn. This is why a zone forms. The upper portions of a support zone and the bottom portions of a resistance zone usually witness short term traders parking themselves there. As you go deeper in the zone, the greater is the presence of higher time frame traders.

When marking these zones on your chart, try to mark them using boxes or multiple lines instead of single horizontal lines. Advanced traders often mark single lines but they understand that those lines represent a zone. As a beginner, it is best for you to remind yourself of this fact as much as possible.

Strength

Support and resistance zones vary in strength as I've mentioned. What are some of the tell-tale signs you can watch out for when it comes to strength? The first and most obvious clue is the force with which price approaches the level and the relative force with which it leaves it.

If price approaches a level strongly and leaves it with equal or even greater force, you can consider that zone to be a pretty strong one. Why is this? Examining things from an order flow perspective is instructive. A move that has a lot of force behind it has a large number of traders backing it. If the traders at a support or resistance zone are able to repel a forceful move with even greater force, that's a pretty good show of strength.

The angle with which price moves towards a level is an important clue as to how strong the move is. The steeper the angle, the stronger the move is. Also pay attention to the angle with which price leaves a level. If this angle is more shallow than the angle with which price moved into the level, it's a sign that the traders at the level aren't as strong as the ones pushing price into it.

The nature of the first bar that is formed when price hits a level is also instructive. If it happens to be a full bodied bar with almost no wicks or tails, that's a significant show of strength. The presence of a pin bar at support or resistance is also a great sign of strength present at the level.

A strong level is also one that gets repeatedly tested and still manages to hold. The resistance zone in Figure 8 is an example of this. Notice the gap between the tests of the level. The larger the gap between retests, the stronger the level is. It means that traders remember that level for longer for whatever reason and you can rest assured that if price makes it back there, price is going to react off it.

In the FX market, you will often see huge volatility being introduced once an important announcement comes in. Interest rate announcements or the release of Non-Farm Payrolls reports often causes prices to spike. In such moments, you might see prices move sharply in one direction and then abruptly stop and form a tail or a wick. Figure 9 illustrates just such an instance.

Figure 9: A Strong Reaction

Figure 9 is a daily chart of the NZDUSD. On the left, where the first circle is you can see a bullish bar with a long wick formed. This bar isn't really a pin bar since the body is pretty large. However, notice the size of the bar. Keep in mind this is the daily chart and the huge move up in price was met by bears and price never reapproached it for a long time.

In fact, it spawned a bearish move and price approached it after a period of almost four months. The market remembered the first rejection from that level and after two retests, prices eventually went south. Notice that the only indication of strength we have here is a long bar with a significant wick.

If this bar had not been rejected, it would have been a huge bullish bar. However, the fact that the bears were able to push back and create a wick indicates that the bearish presence at this level is pretty strong. If you were bullish headed into this level, you'd be best off selling before price got there and even playing the bearish side of the market as price reacts from the level.

Higher Time Frames

Another indicator of strength is the presence of a level on the current time frame that is also a level on the higher time frame. In fact, the more higher time frames the level is present in, the stronger it is. Figure 10 is an H4 chart that shows price repeatedly bouncing off a support level.

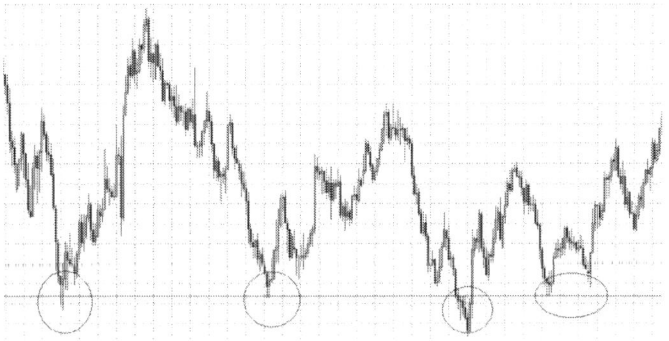

Figure 10: Support on H4

Let's say we're at a point on this chart before the third bounce happens. We've seen two bounces take place already so there is a good chance that a third one might occur. We don't know for sure though. The second bounce left the level at a weaker angle than it arrived and the bounce was far weaker than the extent to which it bounced the first time.

Figure 11 is the same level as it appears on the daily time frame.

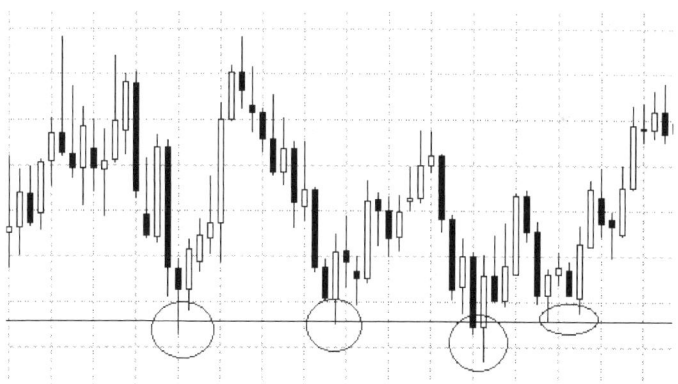

Figure 11: Support on D1 Time Frame

Notice that the level is fully present even in this time frame. You can see that even here, the second bounce looks pretty weak. However, the fact that it is present fully on two separate levels, most importantly on a higher time frame from the one you're trading, indicates that there will be two sets of traders who will be ready to back this level.

This makes the probability of it holding pretty high. Notice how the level seemingly breaks but then finds support and price shoots up. Can we say for sure that the level will always hold? Well, nothing's for sure in the market. Instead, what we can deduce is that the odds of the level holding are high and we should place long trades from it right until it breaks.

You will often see prices travel strongly in a certain direction and then come to a halt and turn on a dime and go the other way. Don't mistake such behavior for a sudden change in trend. What has likely happened is that prices have hit a strong level on the higher time frame and this has caused it to go the other way.

When trading, always keep the higher time frame levels in mind, especially when setting profit targets. If you happen to set one that's just beyond a strong support or resistance one, the odds of prices making it there untroubled are extremely low.

Reversals

By reversals I'm talking about the changing nature of a level and not a price reversal. You will often notice when trading that once price breaks past a certain zone, it uses the zone from the other side to propel itself further. In other words, support turns into resistance when it is broken and resistance turns into support when broken.

Figure 12: Support and Resistance Reversals

Figure 12 illustrates the changing nature of levels and zones. Notice at the top of the chart there is a wide zone that changes from acting as support and resistance depending on which side of it price is on. At the bottom, we have an example of a small resistance level acting as support once it's broken.

These levels are pretty safe bets for you when it comes to place trades. If you see a strong level being broken, it is always a good play to place a trade in the direction of the break and use the level as an entry point. From an order flow perspective, what is really going on here?

Traders tend to switch sides in the market quite a lot. This is because they're always searching for the presence of momentum in the market. The side that has greater momentum always attracts a bigger crowd. When it comes to strong support and resistance levels, traders often line up at these levels since they see the strength present there.

However, if the level breaks, clearly the side that broke the level has greater strength and the majority of traders will now switch sides and will begin to trade from those same levels. This is what causes support to turn into resistance and resistance into support when the zone breaks.

Mind you, it isn't guaranteed that this will always happen. Sometimes, price breaks through so violently that traders don't get a chance to place any orders. In such cases, when price eventually makes its way back, there's no guarantee that the level will act in a reversed role.

However, for any break of a level that is less than violent, you can bank on this happening. It also offers you a quick way to reverse your bias in the market and quickly get in on a profitable trade. This takes a lot of mental strength to do. Having a strong mindset and understanding the principles in the risk management chapter is crucial for you to be able to do this.

Many traders struggle to make switches such as this because they think of trading in the wrong way. Understanding the true nature of trading and managing risk is the solution so pay attention to the material in that chapter when you get there.

Dynamic Levels

The zones that I've highlighted thus far are examples of static support and resistance levels. There are dynamic support and resistance levels as well and the most common form of this is the 20 period exponential moving average or 20EMA. The EMA is a line that connects the closing prices of the last 20 bars. It is plotted on top of price as Figure 13 shows. This is an example of dynamic support.

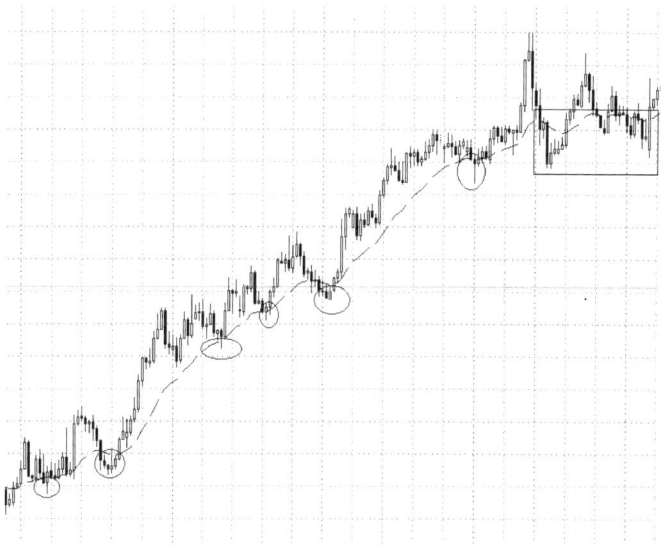

Figure 13: 20 EMA Dynamic Support

The 20 EMA usually functions as a great support or resistance level in the early portions of trends. While you cannot expect prices to bounce neatly off it, notice the number of times prices dip close to it and reverse in its vicinity. What's more, a lot of these instances result in prices throwing almost perfect candlestick patterns for you to enter the trend in.

The problem with dynamic resistance is that when markets become choppy or start going sideways, they tend to fail. Look at the right hand side of this chart and you'll see how the 20 EMA is not being respected anymore. Thus, if you wish to use this as a support or resistance level, you need to make sure that the price environment is right.

As a rule of thumb, as long as you're operating in the beginning of a trend and can clearly see prices moving at a steep angle, you can rest assured that the 20EMA will have some relevance. Remember that much like static support and resistance levels, the 20 EMA is a zone as well.

This is because of the presence of orders from traders operating on multiple time frames. The 20 EMA happens to be the most widely used indicator among professional traders and this is why it is powerful. However, it isn't the only one in use. Some traders prefer the 25 EMA while some prefer the 15 EMA.

This is why you'll see the 20 EMA being pierced before price bounces back through it to continue the trend. Trading dynamic support and resistance can be a bit tricky thanks to you having to predict the approximate safe distance for your stop loss levels. Price tends to crash through these lines a bit and often you will see that prices will hit your stop loss, bounce off those levels and then continue in the direction of the trend.

Don't get frustrated unduly when this happens. You can wait for the bounce back up the 20 EMA line if this happens too many times instead of buying the pair the moment it hits the 20 EMA.

In order to do this well, you need to understand the different types of orders you can use to trade. Let's take a look at these now.

Order Types

A good trader knows what types of orders to use in a given moment. The fact is that using the wrong kind of order can hamper your returns and lose you money. Many traders don't pay enough attention to this part of trading. This is tragic because it really isn't all that difficult to understand how to use orders intelligently.

Market Orders

These are the first type of order you should understand. Market orders are what most traders use to trade, but these aren't always the best option. The default order type your broker will provide you with is a market order. When you place this order, your broker will buy or sell (fill the order) at whatever price the market provides.

For example, if you wish to buy 1.25 units of EURUSD, your broker might fill one unit for 1.234 and the rest at 1.254. Thus, you have no guarantee of the price you're going to receive. With small orders this usually isn't much of a problem since the market always has enough supply to fill your order without moving prices too much.

However, in times of volatility, market orders can lose you a ton of money. You might end up entering your trades at levels that don't make much sense anymore. This doesn't mean to say that market orders are all doom and gloom. You are guaranteed a fill no matter what and you will be in a trade if this is what your choice is.

You should exercise caution with market orders in volatile markets. Sometimes, it's better to trade a smaller position for a good price than enter the full position at a worse price.

Limit Orders

In order to address the deficiencies of market orders with regards to their lack of price protection, limit orders were created. With this order, you are guaranteed execution at a certain price or better. The flip side is you are not guaranteed execution of the entire quantity of your position. Let's see how this works through an example.

If you wish to short 1.25 EURUSD at 1.2345 and place a limit order, your broker will ask you for a trigger price. This trigger price is a threshold. Your broker will execute your order at prices that are equal to or better than this price. The threshold price is also referred to as the 'trigger' or 'limit' price.

In this case, since you're going short, your broker will execute the order only at 1.2345 or greater. Remember that if you're going short, you ideally want high prices on entry so that you can profit from the fall in prices on exit. If your broker manages to find 1.1 units of EURUSD at 1.2346 and no more before market prices decline below the threshold, that is the extent of your position.

Thus, you have a great price, but you do not have the entire position size in place. Limit orders are great in calm markets or when your preferred threshold is high. They work perfectly when you're looking to enter at a support or resistance level as price approaches it. In such trades, you're looking to enter before the price hits the level and bounces off it.

However, if you're looking to enter once a price pattern has been formed, these are not your best choice. By the time a price pattern forms, the market has already begun to run away, and a market order is a better option. All in all, limits are a great order choice in certain situations.

Stop Orders

Limits have an inherent deficiency in them in that you're not guaranteed to fill the entire position quantity. Market orders have a deficiency in that prices can gyrate way too much to guarantee you good trade prices. The stop order seeks to reduce these disadvantages.

Stop orders have triggers as well like limits. However, the difference here is that once the trigger is hit, your broker will execute the order for the entire position size no matter what the market price is. This is extremely helpful when entering the market after a price pattern is formed.

Let's say you spot a bullish pin bar formation and wish to enter immediately. You place a buy stop order with the trigger price equal to the close of the pin bar. As price breaches the trigger, your entire order gets executed at market prices and you are guaranteed a fill.

Stop orders are also extremely useful when you wish to get out of a trade. If prices have gone against you, the overriding aim at that point is to get out of the trade no matter what. You want the position to close and in such situations a limit order is a poor choice since you're not guaranteed a complete fill.

A stop loss order is essentially a stop order. In the case of a long position, the stop loss is a sell stop order while in the case of a short position it's a buy stop order. If you're trading the way this book teaches you to, you will be utilizing stop orders for the most part.

Limit orders have their uses with more advanced techniques that I'll highlight in the next book. You can use market orders but understand that these are risky. You're not guaranteed a price, and neither are you guaranteed a complete fill in volatile markets.

Chapter 5:

Technical Indicators

Indicators are an almost indispensable part of trading. They make the job of figuring out what's going on with regards to price action easy and are good to use in your trading. While price action patterns are great as an entry signal, the fact is that they aren't always present. In such instances, indicators will help you immensely and can function as an alternative means of entering the market.

Despite having been around for many years now and having been used by tons of traders, it is still possible to use indicators intelligently and profitably. The key lies in using them in the right way and not blindly, much as you learned how to do when it came to price action patterns.

This chapter is going to introduce you to four indicators that can be used as strategies themselves or they can be combined with one another to create more strategies. Over and above this, you can also employ price action patterns within them to make them even more effective.

All in all, by the end of this chapter, you're going to have your entry strategy completely sorted out.

Average Directional Index

The ADX is a popular indicator that many traders have used over the years. One of the reasons it is as popular as it is is because it helps traders figure out the strength of the prevailing trend. The ADX can also be used to figure out the direction of the trend but using it in this manner is not something that is recommended. This is partly due to the way in which markets behave when the trends in them lose steam.

As such, the way I'll show you how to use the ADX might seem simplistic, but it is the most powerful method of using it. The simpler your methods are, the easier it will be to implement them. Trading is a fast-paced environment and the easier your decisions are, the better off you'll be.

The indicator itself ranges from values of zero to 100 and is often plotted as a separate window below price. Often, charting platforms will plot two more lines in there called the directional indices. These are indicated with the signs +DI and -DI. You can use the +and - DI to give the ADX a directional bias. If the +DI is above the -DI, the trend is bullish. If the -DI is above the +DI, the trend is bearish.

The moment when the two lines crossover one another is the moment when the trend switches direction. All of this sounds great on paper, but it rarely works out in practice. The fact is that using the DI's will kick you out of trends a lot sooner than usual and you'll end up leaving money on the table.

Even worse you'll end up mistaking a sideways movement in the trend or a small counter trend as being a full blown trend in the other direction and you'll lose money. You should use these only when you have a good idea as to how long trends can last and this is an advanced skill to master. However, when you master that skill you probably won't need the DI's anymore.

Thus, we're left with just the ADX as being relevant. The value of the ADX indicates the strength of the trend that is currently present in the market. Here's what the values mean (Mitchell, 2020):

1. 0-25 - No trend
2. 25-50 - Good trend
3. 50-75 - Strong trend
4. 75-100 - Very strong trend

As you can see from these numbers, anything over 25 is a sign that the trend is good enough for you to enter. The idea behind using the ADX successfully is that once you have a good handle on the strength of the trend, you can use a price action pattern to enter or even enter using a support or resistance level.

When the ADX prints values over 50, you can use dynamic support and resistance to enter. Let's take a look at an example to see how this works.

How it Works

Figure 14: NZDUSD D1 Chart

Figure 14 is a daily chart of the NZDUSD. The ADX is plotted in the window below. A horizontal line in that window indicates the 25 level above which the ADX indicates a strong trend. There is a lot going on in this chart so let me explain all of these first.

In the price chart, you will see three support and resistance levels marked. These are indicated by the letters A, B and C. There are three rectangles indicating sideways market movement that are indicated by the numbers one, two and three. The 20 EMA is also plotted on the price chart and is indicated by the dashed line.

From left to right, the chart clearly shows the NZDUSD in a strong downtrend with a few sideways moves in between. We begin from the left and see that the trend is quite strong and the ADX indicates this as being the case. Values are pretty high and using dynamic resistance to enter into trades is the thing to do at this point.

There are a few pins thrown but generally you could also choose to enter using limit orders with stop losses placed some distance above the EMA. I'd like to point out that you don't really need the assistance of any other indicator to tell you which way the market is headed at this point. Clearly, prices are declining and the ADX is telling you that they're doing so very strongly.

So far, we're in an ideal world where everything is working as it should. However, the sideways movement at 1 starts and everything goes pear shaped. It is at this point that most traders will continue to trade the ADX and will end up making huge losses because they'll trade the wrong environment.

While prices are moving sideways, this doesn't mean the trend is coming to an end. Here's what you need to do. Identify the most important resistance level until this point. The upper boundary of range 1 is this level since this is clearly where the bears are congregating to push prices down. If prices move above this zone, you can switch your bias to bullish.

Until then, you remain bearish and keep watching the ADX for cues as to when the trend will pick back up once again. The market moves into another sideways range at 2. Notice how the bottom boundary of 1 acts as resistance for 2. This level is a great place to look for short entries via price action patterns.

If you're trading using just the ADX, you could sit out this portion of the trend. Eventually, it picks back up and you could enter using dynamic resistance once more since the ADX values spike as price declines.

At the right hand side of the chart, we have a sideways movement at 3 with the upper boundary of 3 functioning as the most important resistance level. As long as the price remains below this level we'll remain bearish. This is also a good zone to look for short entries.

The best way for you to understand how to trade the ADX is to choose what you're to look for prior to trading. Will you use the ADX as your sole entry signal or will you trade the market when the ADX indicates there isn't a trend? My recommendation is to begin by trading just when the ADX indicates a trend.

The in between periods when the market is moving sideways can get tricky since you'll need to abandon the ADX and trade using support and resistance along with price action patterns. Get used to entering a trend when the ADX indicates it is safe to do so. Hence, with this particular chart, you will only trade when the ADX is greater than 25.

When this is the case you can either:

1. Enter at dynamic support or resistance
2. Enter using price action patterns at support and resistance (dynamic or static)

Once you're making money trading this way, you can begin to look for entries when the ADX is not in the picture.

Relative Strength Index

Along with the ADX, the RSI is one of those evergreen indicators that many traders love to use. This is because the RSI is one of the most simple indicators to use and it generates highly reliable signals in the appropriate conditions. The RSI is what is called an oscillating indicator or an oscillator.

This means that it moves between two extreme values that are at 0 and 100. It is plotted in a separate window below the price chart. The RSI window typically indicates two zones within it, with one one occurring near the top of the chart and the other near the bottom.

The upper zone exists between 70 and 100 and is referred to as the overbought zone. The lower zone is between zero and 30 and this is the oversold zone. The idea behind these zones is this. Prices often drift into levels where the instrument becomes overbought or oversold. When this happens the other side of the market seeks to rectify the balance and this causes a swing in the other direction.

By identifying when prices have drifted too much in one direction, the RSI gives you a readymade entry signal that doesn't require any price action patterns or confirmation of any kind. There is one key point you must keep in mind about the RSI though. You need to trade it only when the market is in a sideways movement.

When the market is trending prices will push the RSI into overbought or oversold zones for long periods of time. However, trends occur because one side of the market has a clear advantage over the other. This is why prices rise or fall. Thus, an indication of the market being overbought or oversold is not really relevant in such cases.

In sideways movements though, the markets are more balanced. Another way to think of it is to understand that both sides of the market have equal strength. Therefore, when one side pushes too much, the other side comes right back in and restores equilibrium.

This push and pull in a sideways movement is what the RSI captures and is what you can take advantage of.

How it Works

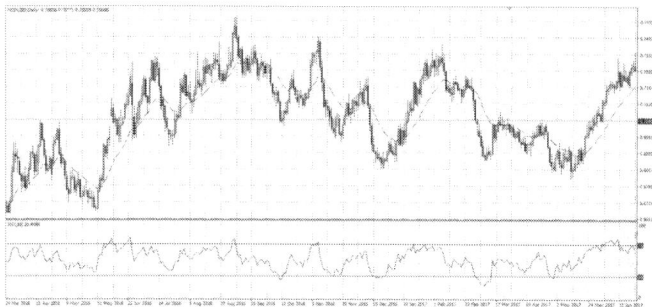

Figure 15: RSI

The chart in Figure 15 is once again of the NZDUSD on the daily time frame. As you can see, this is a sideways movement, but it isn't a completely clean one. The upper and lower boundaries are not very clear. In fact, when looking from left to right, the chart has an upward tilt to it.

These kinds of charts trip up many traders since they aren't sure if this is a trend of a sideways move. The easiest way to figure this out is to either look at the ADX to see whether there is any indication of a trend or to look at how much price fluctuates around the 20 EMA.

You can see that aside from the final right hand side portion of this chart, price bars are evenly distributed around the 20 EMA. They don't really bounce off the EMA nor do they respect it in any way. This is a surefire sign that both sides of the market are exerting themselves equally.

All in all the RSI is the perfect indicator to take advantage of this type of situation. Here's how you ought to trade it. You initiate a long trade when the RSI moves from the oversold zone into the neutral zone. Initiate a short entry when the RSI moves from the overbought into the neutral zone.

A good way to boost the probability of success on these trades is to watch for the presence of a good support or resistance level near your trade entries. In Figure 15, you will see that the short entries have better odds of success since all of the entry signals occur when price is near a resistance zone.

The decision to avoid or enter when you receive signals that are not near a support or resistance level depends on how aggressive you want to be. Contrary to popular perception, aggressiveness has nothing to do with expertise. You can be an extremely profitable trader and be very conservative. It really comes down to how well you can deal with the prospect of losses.

Aggressive traders tend to lose more often but when they do make money, they make quite a lot of it. This causes a higher degree of volatility in their account balances. Mind you, this is not to say that you'll be fluctuating between profits and losses all the time. It's just that your upward move in terms of account balances will be a bit choppy when compared to that of the conservative trader.

However, the slope of the rise in the account balance will be greater for the aggressive trader. All in all, it's a trade-off. There isn't one single method of trading correctly. You can adopt multiple approaches with equal success.

Some traders choose to trade divergences with the RSI. This can be a profitable method of trading the indicator but it's tough to execute in the moment unless you really happen to understand the technique inside and out. For this reason, I recommend only advanced traders use it. However, let's take a brief look at how it works.

The idea behind a divergence is that if the price is displaying different characteristics from what the RSI is printing, there is a chance that this divergence indicates an opportunity. The best way to detect a divergence is to examine the highs and lows price makes as it moves and contrast it to the RSI.

If price makes a new low but if the RSI is well above the oversold zone, this is an indication that price will need to go lower. Thus, a short trade is in order since the RSI tells us that price isn't oversold as yet. Similarly, if price makes a new high but if the RSI isn't in the overbought one, you can enter long since price evidently has to run for a little longer.

Don't think of the overbought and oversold ones as being firm boundaries when trading divergences. For example, the first low that is made in Figure 15 coincides with a trough in the RSI that is slightly above the oversold zone. You might argue that this is a divergence. However, being as close as it is to the oversold zone, this isn't a very high probability divergence and you're better off letting this one go. This is confirmed as price shoots up from this level shortly.

Examining the first swing high from the left is instructive with regards to how divergences work. Price makes a peak here but the RSI is trending lower from the overbought zone. The message here is that prices can rise a little bit longer. Price eventually makes a new peak and a savvy trader could have profited from this.

The problem is that prices declined before shooting up and this is a perfect illustration of why beginner traders will find divergences tough to trade. The decision to time your entry is paramount. The best entry in this case would have been at the minor support level that price dove to before rising up. However, a novice trader's first instinct is to enter the minute they receive a signal.

With divergences you might need to wait a while and plan your trade before entering into it. Do it successfully and the rewards are huge. Do it incorrectly, and you're likely to lose money. My recommendation is to practice trading divergences as much as possible before going live with them.

Follow the path prescribed in the chapter which details how you ought to build your trading plan and use that framework to build your skills. While divergences might be hard to trade they are a profitable strategy that you should use as much as possible. The fact that it's tough to execute is what makes it so profitable since you don't have competition from traders running the same strategy.

All in all, the RSI is a versatile indicator. You can combine it with the ADX to form a strategy that works in both trending as well as ranging markets. You could also use it by itself. The choice is yours. As long as you remember to use it in the right price environments (sideways moves) you'll make money using this.

Parabolic SAR

Unlike the previous indicators that require some assistance from support and resistance or require you to take a step back and assess market conditions, the parabolic SAR (stop and reverse) is a fully built system within itself. This is one of the few indicators you can trust blindly in almost every type of market conditions.

The key to using the SAR well is to pick the right type of instrument instead of the type of environment. Instruments that are extremely volatile don't work well with the SAR for reasons you'll shortly see. While there are a few highly volatile instruments you can use the SAR with, these are best left for advanced traders to deal with.

So what is the SAR? This indicator is superimposed over the price chart directly and is printed as a series of dots either above or below price. The default values for this indicator involve entering a value for the 'step' as well as the 'maximum.' What do these mean?

These can be better understood by understanding the basis on which the SAR was developed. The creator of this indicator reasoned that trends often swing up and down as they head towards their conclusion. The idea was to be able to capture the top or bottom (or as close as a trader could get to them) of these swings so that entries and exits could be timed.

The calculation itself is a bit complex and doesn't really serve any purpose. However, it does contain an element called an acceleration factor that is a number. The minimum, and default, value of this number is 0.02. As a trend accelerates, this increases in steps of 0.02 until it reaches a maximum value of 0.2 (this is the input for the 'maximum' value.)

The higher the step value is, the greater is the acceleration factor and the more sensitive the indicator becomes. As such, you can stick to the default value or even reduce it to a minimum of 0.005. This is because the SAR is used mostly in stable trends and as such, modifying this number isn't going to make all that much of a difference.

After all, the market is headed in a particular direction anyway and you're unlikely to get bitten by a sudden change in direction. Let's look at an example to see how you can make this indicator work for you.

How it Works

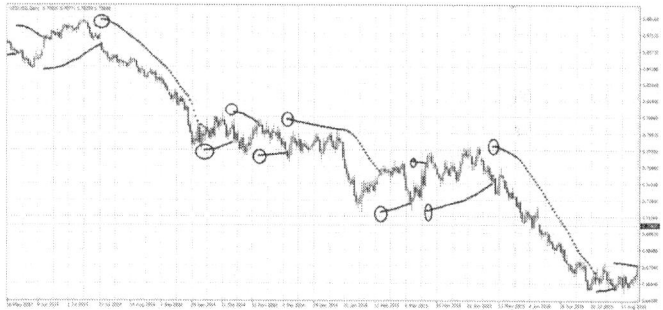

Figure 16: NZDUSD Downtrend

Figure 16 highlights a downtrend in the NZDUSD that I have featured previously. In this chart you can see the Parabolic SAR as a series of dots that are both above and below prices. The circles indicate entry signals as well as exits from the previous trade.

The SAR is an indicator that will keep you invested in the market at all times. You'll be trading against the trend as well and this often causes beginners a lot of problems since they'll often see that the market is headed one way, but the indicator is telling them to go the other way. In strong trends, not all counter trend trades are going to work out. In Figure 16, you can see that almost none of the long trades will result in a profit.

Even if they do result in a profit, the amounts that they yield are very little when compared to the shorts. So, should you ignore the counter trend signals? I would caution against doing this since you might end up sabotaging yourself. In strong trends like the one in Figure 16, it makes sense but in trends that swing around a lot more, you're going to struggle if you try to figure out which signal is valid or invalid.

Thus, the best way to trade this indicator is to adopt the opposite approach from what was discussed with the other ones. Instead of trying to figure out which signals are valid, you simply need to trade every signal there is. Over the long run, you'll find that you'll make a profit.

A word of caution though. You need to apply this indicator in trending markets. Ranging markets will wreak havoc with this system since you'll find that the SAR will flip up or down every two bars or so and you won't have enough time to get in or out. Even worse, you'll end up overtrading and your broker is going to love all the commissions you'll generate for them.

So, what is the best way to ensure you're trading in the right environment? First off, remember that you need to pick the right instrument. To do this you will need to observe the long term price movements in a bunch of instruments. For example, the EURUSD is highly unsuited for this strategy since it tends to move in clusters of sideways movements.

What I mean is that even in a trend, the EURUSD forms large sideways movements, with little trends in between them. This means you won't have enough time to enter and exit. Instead, look for instruments that trend in a smooth manner, whenever they do so. Don't try to look for instruments that trend all the time; this is unrealistic.

Instead, look for a smooth curve and preferably one that lasts for a long time. A great way to help narrow down such instruments is to use the ADX. Look at how long the ADX stays above 25, when the instrument begins to trend. Does the indicator look extremely choppy and does it move to either side of 25 when the price begins to trend? If so, this is unsuitable for the purposes of the SAR.

Even when you pick an instrument, it's best to pair this with the ADX to confirm that you are trading in the right environment. Using the ADX might kick you out of a few profitable early trend signals but the higher degree of accuracy later on will make up for it.

A key issue to take note of with this strategy is the issue of stop loss placement. Here again you can adopt an aggressive or a conservative option. The aggressive option would be to place the stop loss above or below the previous bar. The conservative option would be to place it above or below the closest support or resistance. Keep in mind that if you're in a strong trend, dynamic resistance is also a valid zone to place your stops above or below.

If you find scenarios where placing the stop above or below the previous bar is not feasible, then you must default to the closest support or resistance zone. By using the ADX to help you spot trends, you will increase your success rate but don't expect it to be foolproof or to be right 100% of the time.

Being right and making money have a very tenuous relationship when it comes to trading. You can be wrong with most of your trades and still earn a profit. I'll explain this in detail in the chapter on risk management. For now, just keep in mind that your aim is not to be right but to find systems that give you some form of correct signals.

All in all, the SAR and ADX combination is a great beginner strategy to employ since it involves very little discretionary inputs. You simply look at what your indicators are telling you and you enter. You exit when the indicator flips to the other side and only enter in the opposite direction as long as a trend is on (as indicated by the ADX.)

Bollinger Bands

Like the SAR, which is a system unto itself, Bollinger bands are also a complete trading system that has been seemingly built for the newbie trader. However, the representation of the bands on a price chart tends to look extremely complex and for this reason many new traders are scared away.

The indicator also uses statistical terms that don't make sense to everyone and as a result, this system is underused. All of this is great news for you. The truth is that despite all of this jargon, the bands are a relatively easy system to use. What's more, you can use them in multiple ways.

If you were to examine two experienced traders who are well versed with Bollinger bands, you'll find that they trade it very differently. Thus, the manner in which you choose to trade them is entirely up to you. This means your system will likely be unique in the markets and as such you won't have to worry about anyone riding your coattails.

The bands themselves are represented as an envelope around price. You will typically see three lines on the price chart, superimposed over the price bars. There will be an upper layer, a line that runs through the middle and a bottom layer. The line in the middle is simply the 20EMA.

You can change the period of the moving average to anything else that makes sense to you. Generally, the 20 period is the best choice. The upper layer is a representation of three standard deviations of price movement above the 20 EMA while the bottom layer is three standard deviations below the 20 EMA.

So what does standard deviation mean? As the 20 EMA is plotted, its values will vary from one another. This distribution of numbers will have an average (mean in statistical terms). The standard deviation is a number that expresses the degree by which individual numbers in that group differ from the mean, on average. If this is making your head spin, don't worry, you don't need to fully understand statistical definitions to trade this system.

The envelopes indicate areas where price is unlikely to go beyond. This is because in the short term, a three standard deviation move is highly unlikely. Therefore, you can think of these bands as being price envelopes within which all movement is contained. The best part of the bands is that they take volatility into consideration as well since the standard deviation number will reflect the existing volatility in the market.

How it Works

Figure 17: NZDUSD Downtrend

Figure 17 is the same downtrend in the NZDUSD as before. You can see the bands plotted above and below prices with the 20 EMA in between. There are two ways of trading the bands and you can choose either one of them or choose to trade both in a single system.

The first method is to wait for price to hit the outer envelopes and place a trade in the opposite direction. If price hits the higher envelope, you place a short and if price hits the bottom envelope, you place a long trade. The key to remember with this is that you should be placing such trades only in sideways movements.

Doing this when the price is heavily trending will ruin you. You can see in Figure 17 how prices hug the bottom envelope during the trending phases. Placing long trades under these conditions is not a smart thing to do. However, notice during the sideways movements that prices bounce off the outer envelopes. These entries have been indicated by rectangles in Figure 17. Notice that we place these trades only when the price movement is sideways.

The second way to trade the bands is to use the 20 EMA. This is simply another way of using the EMA as dynamic support or resistance. In strong trends, any price movement towards the EMA is going to result in a move in the opposite direction. These entries have been indicated by circles.

You can combine these two methods to form a system that is valid in almost any market condition. The question is: How do you know whether you're in a range or a trend? The best way is to look at the price chart but if this is too advanced for you, you can use the ADX's values to help you figure out the current state of the market.

All in all, Bollinger bands are a versatile way of trading the market. There's a lot going on in Figure 17 so make sure you study it at your leisure to see the rationale behind some of the entries. The best method of doing this is to cover the bars with a piece of paper and move the paper forward, one bar at a time.

This concludes our look at technical indicators and indeed, all forms of entry methods. You now have a number of techniques to choose from. You can use candlestick patterns, technical indicators or even support and resistance to figure out when and where to enter. It's now time to look at how you should structure your exits, unless the trading system already specifies it.

Chapter 6:

Risk Management for Beginners

I've been going on about risk management quite a bit and now, here we are, finally! Risk management is the other peg upon which your trading success will be built. Many traders think trading successfully is all about spotting the best entries and then placing trades.

This isn't true at all. In fact, it is just half the picture. There is an entire world of risk management that these traders miss and as a result, their bottom lines suffer. The best place to begin understanding trading risk management is to examine how we've been conditioned to expect and define success.

Win Rates

Here's a hypothetical scenario: Below you have information regarding two traders. The question is, who do you think is going to be more successful?

1. Trader X who is correct 95% of the time
2. Trader Y who is correct 25% of the time

Take your time to think this through. Another way of asking this question might be to ask you who would you rather be? Would you rather be right about the market's direction 95% of the time or 25%? Being right in this sense is to make money, since this is how a trader's performance is calculated. So, what we're saying here is that X makes money 95% of the time while Y makes money 25% of the time.

Is your answer ready? Did you pick trader X as the one who is more likely to be successful? If you're like most beginners, you probably did. Well, the fact is that you're wrong. This is a trick question. I haven't given you enough information to be able to make an informed decision as yet.

Before we get to the answer, let's take a look at why you automatically picked trader X.

Linear Thinking

We're conditioned since childhood to think in a linear manner. We attend school and here, we're subjected to a bunch of tests and examinations. The more number of questions you answer correctly, that is the higher the number of times you're correct, the higher is the grade you receive.

This goes on all the way from elementary school through college. The whole time, you're focused on getting the maximum number of questions answered correctly. The best way to do this is to study as hard as possible so that you have enough information. The more information you have, the more you know and the greater are your chances of being correct.

The more correct you are, the higher is your grade, the better is your GPA, and your job prospects increase proportionately. For close to 18 years, we're conditioned in this manner thanks to our education systems. We're told that success equals being right as much and as often as possible.

With all these beliefs in our heads we arrive into the adult world and discover that the world doesn't actually function in this manner. You can do all the right things and still be wrong and unsuccessful. Successful results seem to depend on you getting everything correct. If you get even a single thing wrong, you've failed.

For example, an engineer designing a bridge needs to get all of the elements right. Getting things 90% correct still results in the bridge collapsing. What increases the frustration we feel is that we look around and see people who do all the wrong things and work half as hard as we do, or don't work at all, and achieve far higher degrees of success than we experience.

Most adults chalk this up to the world being unfair but the truth is that we're just not conditioned to understand the system we live in properly. We keep defaulting to the 'get X number of question right' model of success when in reality, the number of questions you answer correctly is just one half of the equation.

The same applies to trading. When you were studying all of the technical indicators previously, how often did you look at price charts to see how often the indicators correctly predict price movements? How often did you tell yourself that the indicator is terrible and that you need to find something else to base your trading systems on?

Quite a bit, I'll warrant. In doing this, you were again defaulting to the thought pattern that has led you to believe that being right most of the time is what defines success. This is also what caused you to pick trader X in the question I asked you previously. You never stopped to consider that you don't have enough information to make an intelligent decision in the first place.

So, what's going on here? What information do you need to complete the picture?

Success and Failure

A trader's success or failure is determined by the amount of money they make in the markets. Annual results are the ones that matter the most, but truth be told, a lot of successful traders have entire years where they lose money. Let's return to our fictional traders X and Y. Consider the following sequence of trades both of them have based on their success rates. Who would you rather be now?

X - 1,1,1,1,1,1,1,1,1,-15 =($6)

Y - -1,-1,-1,-1,-1,-1,-1,-1,5,5 = $2

Over 10 trades, X is correct 95% of the time which means they're right approximately nine times out of 10. They make $1 every time they're right but the one time they're wrong, they end up losing $15. This means they end up with a loss of $6 after 10 trades.

On the other hand, Y is right 25% of the time which means they make money on just two trades out of 10. When they do make money, they make $5 per trade and lose $1 per trade when they're wrong eight times out of 10. Thus, they end up with an overall profit of $2.

This means Y is the more successful trader when compared to X despite being wrong most of the time. So, who would you rather be? My point here is that the average win and loss is just as important to take into account as is the win rate. In plain English, it isn't just about the number of times you're correct. The amount by which you're correct as compared to the amount by which you're wrong also matters.

Trader X is correct quite a lot but fails to drive home the advantage when this is the case. When they're wrong, they ignore the need to minimize their losses and as a result, end up losing money. Trade Y on the other hand is wrong most of the time. However, when they get it right, they make sure to really drive home their advantage.

There are a few conclusions you can draw from this. The first is that success isn't a right or wrong sort of thing. Instead, it exists on a spectrum. Notice that trade X can be successful as well if they just manage to reduce the amount by which they lose. Alternatively, if trade Y wins less during the times they're right, they will end up losing money.

The bottom line is that there are many combinations of win rates and average wins/losses that will make you money and ensure you're successful. This is why I mentioned previously that trading success isn't about the number of times you're right versus the times you're wrong.

You can be wrong most of the time and still make money. Making money is just a function of basic arithmetic. For every win rate that exists, there is a reward to risk ratio that determines whether or not you'll make money. Calculating this is pretty straightforward and doesn't need any specialized formulas.

Simple extrapolate results over 10 trades as we did with traders X and Y and figure out which reward to risk ratio will make sure you break even (zero profit or loss.) The reward to risk ratio is simply the average win divided by the average loss. In the case of trader X, this ratio is 1/15. In the case of trader Y, this is 5/1.

So how do you calculate a breakeven reward to risk ratio? You begin with the success rate. Let's say you have a 40% success rate, which means you win four trades out of 10. Let's assume your average loss is R (which is just a variable we're randomly assigning to signify this amount.)

If you're right on 40% of your trades, this means you'll be incorrect on 60% of them which is to say you'll lose six out of 10 trades. This means you'll lose 6R in total over these many trades. This means that in order to breakeven, you will need to make at least 6R over four trades. Divide six by four and we have a multiple of 1.5R per win.

Therefore, your break even reward to risk ratio is 1.5R (or 1.5/1). As long as your average wins are 1.5 times your average losses, you won't lose money over the long term. When looking for exits for your trade, you need to make sure your wins are at least this amount.

Once you've figured out the combination of win rate and reward to risk ratio that will make you money, it's time to understand some other principles.

Consistency

The first thing you will do after entering a trade is to place a stop loss order. The distance from the stop loss level to your entry is the risk distance. In other words, if prices travel this distance in the opposite direction of your trade, you will lose money. The amount of money you want to lose is R.

So the question is: How do you determine your position size? In other words, how do you determine how many units of an instrument to buy or sell so that if the trade hits your stop loss, you will lose R? This is pretty simple. You simply divide R by the distance between the stop loss and entry and you'll receive the number of units to buy or sell.

Given that FX calculations involve exchanging currencies, you're best off utilizing the calculator I previously highlighted when I discussed calculating position size. Your objective is to keep R as consistent as possible. Let's say you fix R as being two percent of your overall account capital.

This means that every single trade you place you must risk this amount exactly. Not more, not less. Why is this so? The simple answer is that by keeping it consistent you'll ensure that the basic math of profitability you calculated in the previous section will hold up (Kenton, 2020).

Let's say you've landed on a success rate of 40% and a reward/risk ratio of 2R. You've also fixed R as being two percent of your account. If you risk three percent instead for a few trades, you've changed the value of R in your profitability equation. Let's say you risk 3% for six trades and 2% for four. This means your average R per trade is now 2.6%.

Even worse, what happens if you lose some of those 3% trades? Your average loss has now increased. Let's say you lose all six of the 3% trades and make 2R on the four trades where you risked 2%. Your total losses are 18% while your gains are just 16%. In other words, you've lost money.

This has happened solely because you risked too much on those six trades. If you had risked 2% on those six trades, you would have lost 8%. Your gains on the other trades would have been 16%. This would have resulted in a gain of 8%.

Thus, by risking just one additional percent on those four trades, you've created a swing from a profit of 8% to a loss of 16%. Can you see how this loss has nothing to do with your trading system or which technical indicator you use? It all comes down to how well you've managed your risk when trading.

Keep your R consistent. This is the most basic principle of sound risk management. The second point is to ensure you take profits at a level that is at least greater than the break even profit multiple. In the case of a 40% win system, this is 1.5R. As long as you're taking profits at at least 1.6R, you're making money. Do not take profits below this level since you'll once again be throwing the profitability math off kilter.

With this much being said, it's now time to look at an obvious question that will rise. What should R be? In other words, what is the ideal amount of money you ought to risk per trade?

Risk of Ruin

The risk of ruin is a complex statistical principle. Perhaps the best way to explain it is to examine a coin toss. In this case, you can call either heads or tails. In other words, you have a 50% risk of ruin since half the time, you're going to lose. However, this number assumes that you'll be risking everything you have on a single toss.

What if you reduce this amount? What is the risk of ruin then? This is precisely where the complexity comes in, and along with them come the statistics PhDs. As traders, we're not concerned with how his formula is calculated. We're far more interested in what it means.

The risk of ruin measures your chances of losing money. That much is evident in its name. As long as your chances of losing money are zero, it stands to reason that you'll be making money. The best way to calculate this is to use a risk of ruin calculator. The best one is available at https://www.wisdomtrading.com/risk-drawdown-ruin-calc/.

This calculator has the following inputs:

- 'Prob. Win' - This is your win percentage. In our example form previously this was 40% or 0.4 for this calculator.
- Win/Loss ratio - This is the reward to risk ratio. In our case it is two.
- Risk amount - This is the percentage of your account you will risk per trade. Let's fix this at two percent for now.
- Number of periods - This is the number of trades you wish to project the calculations over. Let's fix this at 1,000.
- Loss level - This is the maximum percentage of your capital you want to lose over the number of periods specified previously. Let's fix this at 10% since this is an acceptable amount to lose as a worst case scenario over 1,000 trades.

This gives us a risk of ruin of 36% and a risk of drawdown of 100%. Let's not worry about the drawdown at this point and just focus on the risk of ruin. 36% is a pretty high number. Remember that in order to guarantee that you will make money, you need to fix this at zero percent.

It turns out that 0.25% is the value that produces a close to zero percent risk of ruin. Thus, your R must be fixed at 0.25% of your account capital. If you have $2,000 to trade, you should be risking $5 per trade. This seems like a ridiculously low amount and you might be wondering how on earth you'll be able to make any money by risking this amount?

After all, if you follow the profitability math, you'll be making $10 per trade. This hardly moves the needle. I'll address these questions in detail in the mindset chapter. For now, remember that if you're risking anything above your risk of ruin determined risk percentage per trade, you're increasing your chances of losing money.

Not many beginner traders will heed this advice since pretty much everyone enters trading with thoughts of making large amounts of money in a short time. It can happen for you. It's just that the means of doing this are not what you think they are. The way to make millions in trading is to keep your risk of ruin at zero percent at all times.

I must mention for the sake of completeness that not all traders subscribe to the risk of ruin model. I'm not talking about traders who are greedy but traders who are professionals and know what they're talking about. Instead, these traders tend to place a greater deal of weight on the profitability aspect of trading and tailor their per trade risk levels to match their own simulations.

Ultimately, it comes down to where you land with regard to the theory behind the risk of ruin formula. The debate affects trading principles, but it isn't something that a trade should immerse themselves too deeply in when starting out. I'll say this instead: If the risk of ruin isn't to your liking then fix your risk to a level where you can take 20 losses in a row safely and still maintain mental composure.

For example, if you decide to risk 2% per trade and lose 20 trades in a row, you'll lose 40% of your account. On a $2,000 account this amounts to $800. Can you remain mentally stable and still believe in your trading system after such huge losses of capital? Will you give up and try to find some other system? If the answer is yes, then you're risking far too much.

Reduce your per trade risk down to a level where you can sleep at night and not make harsh judgments about yourself. You might say that you don't want to lose 20 trades in a row to begin with, but the fact is that the outcome of the trade is not in your hands. You will hit losing streaks and you are going to have to deal with them.

This is why it is crucial that you take the time to properly determine your per trade risk levels.

Amount or Percent

Another debate that often crops up when it comes to per trade risk is to ask whether you're better off risking a particular amount per trade or a fixed percentage of your account per trade. I'll say this much: Those that risk a fixed amount per trade have never traded in a professional setting in their lives.

This is because a fixed amount risk model does not lend itself to any form of statistical measurement whatsoever. Your risk and reward amounts will be fixed but your account balance will experience extreme volatility. If a professional trader trading a bank's money or a hedge fund's money produced these kinds of results, they wouldn't last very long.

The primary argument of the fixed amount model is that it helps the trader recover from losses faster. For example, if your account capital is $2,000 and you're risking 2%, your per trade risk is $40. Let's say you lose one trade. This brings your account capital to $1,960. Your new per trade risk is $39. Let's say you win this trade at a multiple of 2R. Your new balance is $2,038.

How would this look in a fixed amount model? Let's fix the per trade risk amount at $40 once again. After your first loss, your account balance is $1,960. After your first win, it jumps to $2,040. You've made an additional $2 which is close to one percent over two trades. Over 100 trades, you'll likely make 100%!

Obviously, a fixed amount model works better right? Well, not quite. The major flaw in this system is that it ignores the downside risk. Let's say you lose your second trade instead of winning it. Here's what the account balance would look like after two trades:

- Fixed percent model - $1,921
- Fixed amount model - $1,920

The gap between the two models on the downside will only increase since the fixed amount will represent a far greater proportion of the account in terms of percentage. You'll lose money faster. You might argue that you make money faster as well with the fixed amount model.

However, the fact is that you cannot predict in advance which trade is going to make you money and which one is going to lose. If you've lost ten trades in a row risking $40 per trade, that's a $400 loss you've incurred. Will you be willing to risk $40 with an account balance of $1,600?

What happens if you lose 20 trades in a row? You've now lost $800 and your account balance is down to $1,200. In the fixed risk percent model, you'd end up with $1,345 after losing 20 trades while risking two percent. That's a 12% difference in account capital. While the situation is still bad, it isn't as bad as it is in the other scenario.

Traders who risk fixed amounts per trade end up changing their risk amounts after a string of losses. Even worse, they increase their amounts after a few wins. This means that when they do lose, they accelerate their loss curves despite winning a few trades in a row. This captures the worst of all worlds.

As a final word: There is no way you can calculate your risk of ruin using a fixed amount model. In order to be successful you need to risk a fixed percentage of your capital in a disciplined manner.

This discussion might leave you wondering as to how you're going to make big money. After all, if you're going to make just $10 per trade, it's going to take you a long time to make anything worthwhile. This is where your mindset comes into the picture.

Chapter 7:

The Trading Mindset

Everyone gets into trading for the huge money on offer but almost everyone has the wrong notions of what this looks like. They think that all they have to do is place a few trades and they'll make millions per year in profits. Well, it doesn't quite work like that. The fact is that the amount of money you make in trading is directly proportional to your capital and to the number of trades you place as a part of your system.

Before taking a look at either of these though, it is important to lay the foundations of a proper trading mindset and in the process clear some misconceptions of what trading is all about.

Why Trading?

While everyone wants to trade to make big money, the circumstances in their lives are very different. Some people look to augment their regular income with trading while others seek to replace it completely. Some more, quit their jobs and try to make trading a full-time scheme.

Whatever your reason for wanting to trade might be, understand that as long as you feel that you 'have' to make money from the market, you will not be successful. This is because trading a mental endeavor and in order to succeed, you need to create an environment where your mind is as stress free as possible.

If you're relying on trading to pay your heating bills, odds are good that you're going to spend the month freezing away in your home. A lot of traders try to predict their trading success in terms of a monthly return or a yearly return. The reality is that trading doesn't work this way (Kenton, 2020).

Professional traders have consecutive years where they lose money. Being professionals and being added to the markets, these people place thousands of trades every year. Ask yourself: Can you stick to the course and continue to have confidence in yourself if you ended up losing money for two years straight?

Will you still believe in your trading system or will you think that you need to find something better? A system that is more 'correct' and so on? A lot of traders have flawed expectations of what it means to be a successful trader, and this ends up costing them a lot of money and time. Even worse, they end up quitting trading at the wrong times. They mistake a losing streak for failure.

The financial news is full of topics dealing with the annual returns of hedge funds and other investment vehicles. Take a look at some of the most successful investors of all time and their investment records. You will notice that despite earning outsized returns overall, they have years where they lose significant amounts of money.

In the face of this, expecting a steady monthly amount of returns as if it were a salary is unrealistic. Trading is a business like any other and there isn't a business on the planet that can predict its future returns with any kind of accuracy.

Therefore, the first thing to take stock of is your expectations.

Expectations

A surefire sign of a mindset that is going to result in failure is projecting returns and mentally buying all sorts of luxury goods with these projected gains. The average unsuccessful trader has bought millions of dollars worth of real estate and fancy cars in their heads. All the while, their bank account continues to dwindle, and they just can't figure out what's going wrong.

They constantly tinker with their system and in most cases, have no clue what their profitability ratios are. Even if they do know them, they don't practice good risk management that ensures they'll make money. The increasing losses cause all sorts of mindset issues and ultimately the trader loses confidence and ends up either quitting trading entirely or continues to search for that elusive perfect system.

One of the fears that comes into direct opposition with inflated expectations is the fear of losing money. Money is an emotional topic for all of us and almost every single one of us has some sort of harmful thoughts about it. Perhaps you grew up in a poor household or you grew up in a household where money was present, but it was treated as being scarce.

Still some more of us grew up in homes where our parents were profligate with money and as a result, we either adopted their behaviors or we rebelled and went the other way, being extremely conservative with it. Whatever your issue is, it often results in us attaching meaning to the presence or absence of money in our lives.

In the midst of all this comes trading where money is won and lost every single day. You could begin your trading session by losing ten trades straight and still end up making money. Alternatively, you could win ten in a row and lose money in the session. All of this can happen despite practicing great risk management.

It is extremely tough for a beginner trader to keep their composure under such circumstances since they'll attach a huge degree of meaning to every single trade. One of the ways of reducing this need to make money is to go back and view the risk management principles you learned.

In the previous chapter we contrasted traders X and Y and their degree of success. Here's a question. Let's say the math as it was presented for trader Y holds up. What would be the easiest way for them to make more money? There are three ways:

1. They could reduce their average loss size
2. They could increase their average win size
3. They could simply place more trades.

The first two options involve tinkering with the underlying profitability metrics. By changing these, they will change their R values as well as create side effects on their win rates. These could lead to complications. Instead, why not simply place more trades? They know that the math works out over ten trades. It will obviously work over 1,000.

In the real world of trading, the distribution of your wins and losses are unpredictable. You could lose 10 in a row and win 10 in a row. This makes the long term even more important. Instead of focusing on the result on a single trade, focus instead on your results after 1,000 trades. Save judgements about your ability after placing 1,000 trades instead of evaluating yourself after every single trade.

If you find yourself becoming emotional after every single loss or win, odds are that you're still thinking in terms of 'being right equals success.' Remember that this is incorrect when it comes to trading.

Another interesting way to look at this need to be right all the time is to evaluate whether you should even care about a solitary result. After all, if your odds hold up (40% wins with 2R reward/risk ratio) you will make money. It is impossible not to. If this is the case, why should you even care about what an individual trade's result is?

You can literally set your trade and forget about it. The result doesn't matter in the least.

Fear of Missing Out

FOMO is a big one when it comes to trading. It leads to all kinds of problems such as revenge trading and feelings of worthlessness. This fear arises primarily because of the need to make money no matter what and connecting that to your sense of self-worth. This leads to you placing undue amounts of pressure upon yourself even before you've begun trading.

You'll end up counting the gains you missed and you'll constantly feel as if you're not doing a good job. How could you? Your brain is constantly telling you that you need to be perfect when it comes to trading. You need to take every single entry correctly, execute everything perfectly and exit at just the right moment over and over again.

I'm not saying these things are impossible to do. It's just that expecting yourself to do all of these things when starting out is impossible. You will make mistakes and this is how you'll learn how to execute better. The problem is that your fear of missing out will magnify every mistake you make and will make it seem as if trading successfully is an impossible task.

A huge part of trading successfully is preparation. The thing with preparation is that it takes time, a lot of which is spent away from the market. Here's a quick question for you: Do you think you can be a successful trader if you take regular breaks from the market? If you replied 'no' then you will likely suffer from some form of the fear of missing out when you begin trading live.

Trading places a great deal of stress on your mind and you need it to function at a high level in order to be successful. Your mind and brain cannot possibly be at peak levels throughout the year. You will experience burnout and will need to take breaks away from the market. What's more, you will also need to take time to work on and enhance your skills. You will need to take time off in order to review all the things you've been doing and pinpoint areas that need improvement.

Doing all of these things goes against the model of steady monthly income that many beginners build in their minds. After all, if you need to take a month away from the markets to regroup and recover from burnout, doesn't that mean you'll not make any money that month? While it's true that you won't make any money, thinking that you need to trade all the time to make money hardly makes sense either.

A side effect of the fear of missing out is giving into the tendency to revenge trade. You miss one trade and beat yourself up. You now feel the need to make up for that loss and end up taking the next trade setup whether it was perfect or not. The trade goes for a loss and now, in your mind, you've endured a double setback.

Not only did you miss a profitable trade, you endured a loss as well. This puts immense pressure on you and it takes a lot of effort to remain as objective as possible for your next trade.

The best way to remove this fear is to eliminate all need for you to rely on the markets for income. Be prepared to lose your entire capital and ensure that you're trading with money you will not miss. This piece of advice is provided by all trading books, but my point in offering it here is that, unless you do this, your chances of success are minimal.

Do you want to trade or do you want to trade successfully? The choice is yours.

Habits

Examining your habits is a great way to both take stock of as well as fix whatever's going wrong inside your head when it comes to trading. Your beliefs about money and success will reflect themselves in the habits you undertake as you go about your day. When it comes to trading, beginners feel that the only habit to keep in mind is the action of sitting down to trade and analyzing the markets.

However, the fact is that your trading routine begins much before you ever sit down to trade. The amount of importance you give your trading business is reflected in the time you take to prepare for it and in how much priority you give it.

Let's examine these one by one.

Preparation

This is perhaps the biggest and most important of all phases as it relates to trading. It begins right when you go to sleep the previous night. The quality of your sleep determines how refreshed you'll be the next day. Would you rather analyze markets half asleep or do you think you'll do a better job if you've slept well and are completely refreshed? The answer is obvious.

Despite this a lot of traders do not prioritize preparation. They think that rolling out of bed to sit and trade is a perfectly acceptable thing to do. When it comes to forex, this behavior gets worse. Due to the 24-hour nature of the market you can literally fire up your trading terminal at any point in time and place trades.

This leads to a lot of traders simply placing trades on a whim or on the basis of some crackpot economic theory they have. This sort of indiscipline is unlikely to make you any money over the long run, even if you manage to make a few bucks here and there in the short run.

Stick to your strategy and know exactly what you're looking for. Even if your strategy is really simple and mechanical, make sure you're present at your desk at least 30 minutes before your trading session begins. Use this time to catch up on whatever has been going on and to get into the mindset that you need to trade successfully.

A good way of trading the FX market is to trade the four hour charts over the course of the day. This way, if you have a full-time job, you can work at it and check in every four hours to see how things are going. In such situations I recommend checking in at least 15 minutes prior to the end of the current four hour bar. This way, you'll have ample time to be able to catch up on whatever has happened.

Preparation also involves practicing your skills. Your strategy will require you to master certain skills. How well do you know them and how well are you improving them? How much time are you dedicating everyday to practice these skills? Do you really think you can learn thm just once and then start applying them in the markets?

For example, how well can you identify pin bars and the optimal trading conditions to use them in? What about those borderline cases where the tails or wicks are not as long as you'd like them to be? What is your plan for such situations? Practice sessions are where these come to light. In the beginning, all you're going to be seeing is borderline cases of pin bars, so practice is essential.

Set aside at least 30 minutes everyday to practice your skills. Also take as much time as you need to prepare to trade. If you feel harassed or stressed out, do not trade. You'll only end up losing money.

Post-Trade Behavior

Once your trade is close for either a profit or a loss, how do you behave? What are the words you tell yourself and what statements do you make? If you lose, do you think you've failed somehow? Here's the thing: You have zero control over the movement of prices.

This is because prices are controlled by the whims and opinions of other traders. There are millions of traders at any given point in the markets. The average person struggles to get even one person to do exactly what they want them to do. Why do you think you can somehow control a million to do what you want? If you are disappointed that the trade went for a loss, isn't this what you're believing?

The same applies if you make money on a trade. Be happy that you made money by all means but recognize what you did right instead of focusing on the profits. Pat yourself on the back for executing your trade and for risking the correct amount of money. Don't congratulate yourself for being a genius for making a certain amount of cash.

Even when it comes to losing trades, recognize that the actions that precede a perfectly executed losing trade and a perfectly executed winner are exactly the same. The only difference is the opinion of other traders and you cannot control that. Thus, rejoice in your own actions and in executing what you can control.

You need to break the link between success and the outcome of your trade. Remember that you can do everything right for most of the time and still lose money. Being right and being successful are two different things and one does not imply the other.

Understand that there are always things for you to learn from your winners and losers. Journal and examine your trades to spot areas you can improve. Spend time on the weekends reviewing the screenshots of your trades as well as your actions in the lead up to the trade entries. Maintain your journals rigorously.

A good idea is to jot down all of your thoughts prior to trade entry as well as when your trade has closed. When you review these, take note to see if you can spot any thought patterns you can rectify.

Build these habits into your trading routine and you'll find that you will be successful. Technical skills aren't the only ones necessary to be successful, you need to build your mindset as well as your risk management skills in line with them.

Chapter 8:

Scaling

Like any business, it is not a good idea to jump right in and try to do things on the biggest possible scale in trading. The best approach to take is to ease yourself into it bit by bit so that you'll avoid all sorts of nasty surprises. Trading is a tough endeavor, but a lot of traders make it tougher than it needs to be on themselves.

This chapter is going to give you the perfect scaling plan for your trading. Follow it and your chances of success will multiply greatly.

The First Step

Once you've read this book you will be tempted to try and employ your own strategy in the market and you'll be tempted to try and make some money quickly. This is the wrong thing to do. Instead, you first need to invest money in purchasing a market simulation software.

You have a wide variety of choices when it comes to this. You can invest in a standalone tool like Ninjatrader or Forextester. Alternatively, you can sign up for a demo account with a few brokers who will give you access to the simulator tools within the MT5 trading platform.

MT5 stands for MetaTrader 5 and this is the most widely used trading terminal software in forex. Your broker will give you free access to their demo platform where you will be able to access historical data and test drive your strategies.

The point of simulation is to first train yourself in the technical skills you need and to then test drive your strategy. One of the first technical skills you will need to master is candlestick charting. Then comes support and resistance. Only then should you move onto technical indicators. In other words, follow the order in which they were introduced in this book.

Keep in mind that demo trading is different from simulation. Simulation involves replaying historical market data and recording your results. The program or app will do this for you automatically.

The advantage of simulators is that you can replay years worth of market data in a very short time and you'll be able to figure out what the risk numbers look like for your strategy. Aim to place 1,000 simulated trades across a maximum of two instruments. It's even better to place all these trades in a single instrument.

Go as far back as you can to place this number of trades. Remember that if you go down a time frame, you can increase the number of trades you can place. Since we're dealing with forex, pay attention to the time of the day when these trades are placed. Will you be at the screen when some of them are placed, or not. Discard these if they don't apply.

Over 1,000 trades you will now have a good idea of your win rate as well as your average win and loss size. For starters, aim for a 2R reward to risk ratio. If you find that around the 500 trade mark this ratio isn't making sense, restart and aim for a higher multiple based on whatever win percent you had until that point.

You will need to use your common sense here. Don't make any modifications until you hit the 500 trade mark though and do not proceed to the next step until you've placed 1,000 trades and know your numbers thoroughly.

The Second Step

This is when you'll be demo trading. Demo trading is when you'll be trading the market as it moves in real time but you'll be placing trades on paper. Every forex broker provides demo trading accounts for free, so these are no problem to acquire. Place your trades as if you're trading them live.

Demo trading is for you to determine whether your numbers from simulation still hold or not. Can you replicate the same level of success in the demo environment? Obviously, you won't be able to take 1,000 trades but over the course of a month or two you will be able to get a feel for the way the market is working in real time.

All in all, you should spend at least six months trading in demo mode. If you make money at the end of a consecutive six month period, you're ready to go live. Just to clarify: I'm not talking about making money every single month. I'm talking about the cumulative result of six months of demo trading. If you've made money, even if it is one percent, proceed to trading live.

The Final Step

By the time you'll be trading live you will have been trading in one form or another for at least seven months to a year. You'll understand your chosen instruments well and you'll know what to reasonably expect. Don't begin with more than two instruments at first. This means that in the prior steps you'll be test driving two instruments at the most.

Start off risking the correct amounts when trading live. Live trading usually brings its own cocktail of emotions with it so be careful with the amounts you risk. Rely on your routines to see you through the tough moments.

When it comes to adding new instruments, do so only if you've been making money when trading live. If you find that you've lost money after a six month period, take some time off and examine what you've done differently from the previous two steps. This usually points to some form of mental challenge when trading live money.

If you're adding new instruments then pass them through these same steps. Place 1,000 simulated trades, six months of demo and only then can they go live.

Conclusion

I previously mentioned that you will be risking small amounts of money when trading. The way to make large amounts of money is to expand your portfolio in a controlled manner. At first, you'll be making $10 on a single instrument. This becomes two, then four then eight and so on. You cannot increase your portfolio size indefinitely but you'll find that soon you'll be making more than enough money to earn a good side income.

As you get better at trading, you'll find that your evaluation periods will also become smaller since you'll have enough experience to quickly determine which instruments make sense and which one doesn't for your trading style. All of this is fine, you might be thinking, but how do you make the REALLY big money?

Many brokers these days run trading incubators. If you have a good enough track record, you will be placed in these programs and upon satisfying their requirements you will receive funding as well as be put on a path to becoming a professional trader. The most famous of these programs is run by the analytics company Psyquation.

This platform uses AI to spit out a score for a trader's abilities and funding allocations are made according to that. In addition to this, you could do things the old fashioned way. Have your records audited and send them to proprietary trading firms and other small hedge funds.

Remember that it isn't your absolute performance but your risk adjusted returns that will be evaluated. In other words, your ability to manage risk and keep things consistent in that area is what will be looked at. As a professional trader, receiving capital allocations between one to five million dollars is not uncommon. The gains on those levels of capital while risking 0.25% of your capital per trade will surely be substantial enough to satisfy you.

Trading is not the easiest of endeavors but this is a good thing. If it were easy, everyone would be doing it. There are firms out there looking to find great traders because they're in short supply. You can be one of the great trader success stories! All you need to do is adopt a disciplined approach and keep working on your skills.

I wish you all the luck in the world and do let me know what you think of everything you've learned. If you wish to improve your skills, check out the next book in this series where I'll dive into more advanced forex trading concepts!

References

Chen, J. (2020). Learn About Trading FX with This Beginner's Guide to Forex Trading. Retrieved 30 March 2020, from https://www.investopedia.com/articles/forex/11/why-trade-forex.asp

Kenton, W. (2020). Risk Management in Finance. Retrieved 30 March 2020, from https://www.investopedia.com/terms/r/riskmanagement.asp

Mitchell, C. (2020). Average Directional Index - ADX Definition and Uses. Retrieved 30 March 2020, from https://www.investopedia.com/terms/a/adx.asp

Rolf, R. (2020). Why Most Traders Lose Money – 24 Surprising Statistics. Retrieved 30 March 2020, from https://www.tradeciety.com/24-statistics-why-most-traders-lose-money/

Made in the USA
Las Vegas, NV
19 January 2021